Di

the Lower

Stour

Worldwide travel titles in the *Discover* series in print or in preparation include:

Cyprus & North Cyprus, The Dominican Republic, Florida, The Gambia, Gibraltar, The Grand Canyon State, Hungary, Malta, Morocco, Poland, Sardinia, The Seychelles, Tunisia. (These titles are distributed to the book trade through Roger Lascelles, 47 York Rd, Brentford, TW8 OQP).

Titles on English regions akin to this volume: *Discover The Suffolk Coast* (first published 1976 and republished in this format), *Discover North Norfolk.*

Maps. Ordnance Survey maps 155 and 168 of the Landranger 155 series cover the lower Stour at a scale of 1:50,000, approximately 1.25 inches to 1 mile.

Notes for foreign readers. Before **decimalisation** in 1971, British currency had 12 pennies or pence to a shilling, and 20 shillings to a pound. Six shillings and eightpence was written either 6s 8d or 6/8d and was worth 33p in decimal terms. **B&B** means 'bed and breakfast,' usually available in private houses, farmhouses or pubs (public houses). You will see the sign all over the country and in this book. American readers should note that their 'first floor' is the British **ground floor,** their second the British first.

Cover: Willy Lott's Cottage, now called a 'house,' is the best-known building in the lower Stour.

Discover
the Lower Stour

Terry Palmer

HERITAGE
HOUSE

DISCOVER THE LOWER STOUR

First published August 1975 by Stourdale Press Ltd as *The Lower Stour*
Reprinted May 1976
This edition uses only the basic historical information of that first edition, with all other text re-researched.

This edition, January 1992

ISBN 1.85215.0297

Typesetting by Anglia Photoset, Colchester, from in-house computer setting. Typeface is Rockwell, 8.5 on 9.5.

Printed by Kultura, Budapest, Hungary.

Distributed by Heritage House at 'Lavandou,' Steam Mill Rd, Bradfield, Manningtree, CO11 2QT, ✆0255.870595.
Published by Heritage House (Publishers) Ltd, King's Rd, Clacton-on-Sea, Essex, CO15 1BG.

Acknowledgements.
Stanley Booth, Dedham; Catherine Broome-Lynne, Field Studies Council, Flatford; George Curtis, Dedham; Brenda Gamlin, East Bergholt; L.S. Hartley, Stoke-by-Nayland; Bob Horlock, Mistley; Celia & Paul Jennings, formerly of East Bergholt; Canon Tony Jones, Brantham; Colin Miles, Clare; Charles Rose, Mistley; Lady Sue Ryder, Cavendish; and the staff of tourist offices in Colchester, Dedham, East Bergholt, Hadleigh, Lavenham and Sudbury.

Opinions expressed in this book are the author's except where stated otherwise.

> Entrance fees and opening hours of tourist attractions may change. Before beginning a long journey to see something special, check the current times by phone.

CONTENTS

INDEX of MAPS

120–121

122–123

124–125

Terry Palmer (right) and Dennis Hawes get together again.

Terry Palmer was born on the Cambridgeshire-Norfolk border and moved to Essex in 1970. He has had a lifelong interest in writing, photography, maps, languages and travel, making him a perfect candidate for the role of travel writer. He was a reporter on the *Harwich and Manningtree Standard* when Dennis Hawes suggested to him that 'somebody' ought to write a guide book to Manningtree. Terry and Dennis, with others, wrote and published the guide book themselves, and later founded the Stourdale Press of which they lost control following a major fire in Dedham.

Terry eventually moved on, via the Post Office trade paper, to establish his own publishing company, Heritage House, through which he publishes guides to far-flung destinations.

The story comes full circle as Dennis and Terry get together again to write and publish this much-improved version of the original guide book which topped the Colchester best-sellers list for several weeks in 1975.

1: THE STOUR

A swan's-eye view

THE RIVER STOUR rises in Cambridgeshire. Its main sources are on a deserted World War Two airfield south of the village of Weston Green, between Haverhill and Newmarket, but a score or more of springs along these chalk hills feed the struggling Stour as it heads south-east towards Kedington, its first large village. The baby Stour – pronounced to rhyme either with *your* or *our* – is born above the 350ft (100m) contour close to the highest acre of land in East Anglia, and is one of four English rivers to have this name; the others are in Oxfordshire by Shipston-on-Stour, in Dorset by Sturminster, and in Worcestershire and Staffordshire by Stourport and Stourbridge.

The young East Anglian Stour picks up several tributaries as it comes down off the chalk lands and into the Tertiary soils, laid down around 65,000,000 years ago, but it has passed Clare and Cavendish before it meets its first good stream, the River Glem that comes down past Glemsford. Near Long Melford it welcomes the Chad Brook and now becomes a waterway that occasionally commands respect from mortal man: in rare wet winters the Stour floods the water meadows north of Sudbury and has been within feet of the main road north out of town.

Sudbury. In the days before road and rail quickened the tempo of life, barges came upstream as far as Sudbury; the town's Corporation had an Act of Parliament passed in 1705 giving it the authority to create a 'navigation' and so bring barges up to 45ft (13m) long to Ballingdon, a riverside village that has now been swallowed by the town. The Corporation built locks downstream to Flatford, the lowest point for fording the river regardless of the tide, and trade in bulky commodities such as bricks and grain flourished until the railways came. The **River Stour Trust** was established in 1968 to restore the lower course of the waterway to its former glory, and in 1975 it celebrated its first big triumph by reopening Flatford Lock; since then it has raised a sunken barge at Ballingdon, restored Quay Basin and Gasworks Cut in Sudbury, converted a nearby derelict granary into its headquarters and interpretive centre, and restored Dedham Lock.

The Stour is wider and deeper below Sudbury, though there are stilll those rare occasions when it overflows its banks and spreads across the meadows up to a mile wide but only a foot or two deep. At Higham it takes the waters of the River Brett, coming down from Hadleigh, and within a mile the Stour has gone through another lock and entered Stratford St Mary, a village built on the Roman road from Camulodunum (Colchester) that led into the wilds of eastern Britannia.

Dedham Vale. Stratford is the gateway to Constable's Country, which is not to be confused with the Dedham Vale. The Dedham Vale Society was founded in 1938 to fight the proposed demolition of the Sun Inn's coaching arch. After its success it struggled to win official recognition of the region's charms, but popular opinion was not ready. Then in 1964 a proposal to enlarge East Bergholt, Dedham and Stratford brought a public inquiry and, with the need for conservation established, a Government report led to the designation in 1968 of the lower valley as an area of outstanding natural beauty, an AONB in official jargon, stretching from Nayland to the Cattawade barrage, and this, in its strictest sense, is the Dedham Vale.

Hay Wain. In the parish of East Bergholt the Stour drifts lazily past Willy Lott's Cottage, which the National Trust now calls a 'House,' and so becomes part of England's cultural history, for Constable's picture of the Hay Wain – the 'hay wagon' – must surely be the nation's best-known landscape painting.

Downstream of the Cattawade barrage the Stour is a different river altogether. It is tidal, rapidly widening to more than a mile (2km). At Mistley it can carry coasters up to 1,000 tonnes, but at journey's end, where the Stour meets the Orwell to form **Harwich Harbour,** it floats vessels of more than 15,000 tonnes at Parkeston Quay, Britain's second largest sea passenger terminal, and at Felixstowe, Britain's largest container port.

In just 47 freshwater miles plus nine miles of tideway, the River Stour has graduated from a trickle of water scarcely big enough to splash in, to a feature of the landscape easily recognisable from outer space.

2: TIDEWATER

Manningtree, Mistley, Brantham.

MANNINGTREE is the smallest parish in Essex, and almost certainly the smallest in Britain – unless you know of one smaller. It has 22 acres (8.8ha) at low tide, but only 17 (6.8ha) are uncovered when the tide comes in. It is so small that one end of its short High Steet is in Lawford and the other is in Mistley – and from the crossroads in the middle of High Street you can see both ends. Manningtree market, trading on Saturday, and Manningtree Station are both in Lawford, while Manningtree television transmitter is in Mistley.

Urban parish. This picture of the urban parish helps put it in perspective, for Manningtree is like London in that it grew out of its neighbours and is now the focal point and shopping centre for several miles around, though continually overshadowed by Colchester and Ipswich to south and north.

Manitre. Under the name of Manitre it became a town of considerable importance in the Middle Ages as a 'free burgage' and market town, the Lord of the Manor of Scidinghoo (to use one of several spellings) being granted in 1238 the right to hold a market. In its prime Manningtree also had an annual fair which attracted merchants from a wide area, and at which it was the custom to roast a whole ox. Shakespeare even mentions it in *Henry IV* with his reference to Falstaff as 'that roasted Manningtree ox.' Mr Falstaff himself is based on a 14th-cent character from Cavendish.

The parish stretches southward from the bank of the Stour, climbing fairly steeply for this part of the country and embracing the Methodist and Catholic churches; the site of the Anglican Church; the old Guildhall, restored in the 1970s and now holding an Indian take-away; and four public houses of which the White Hart is most noticeable for its connections with the stagecoaches of bygone days.

Postman's problem. But this boundary is far from easy to locate on the ground, and many longstanding residents of the area are not certain in which parish they live. Two primary schools which disappeared in the 1980s sat astride the boundary with Mistley and, when I wrote the first edition of this book, York Street in Manningtree had its houses numbered 1 to 5 until it reached the boundary with

Mistley, where the numbering started again at 1.

The parish is so small that it has severe administrative problems. There are just seven members on the parish council – it's sometimes difficult to find enough volunteers for the job – and two on the district council.

Catacombs. Not surprisingly, the ecclesiastical parish of Manningtree has long ceased to exist. St Michael's Church was demolished in 1966 because of a severe attack of woodworm, but the congregation had already transferred to Mistley, being served by that village's Church of St Mary, built in 1870-'71. St Michael's, dating from 1616, was one of the few in England to be built in Jacobean style, and its weathervane went to that other St Michael's in Brantham, the organ to Colchester Royal Grammar School, and its Constable painting of *The Ascension* to the church at Feering, Essex. In 1974 the catacombs were opened by workmen redeveloping the site – and the last lead-lined coffins of the local Alston family were revealed, to be reburied in Manningtree's section of Mistley cemetery.

Playground gravestones. Oddly, Manningtree still had a cemetery in 1974, but it had been covered with tarmac to become the playground of one of those schools I mentioned, with the headstones forming a bizarre boundary. They've now been catalogued and moved.

WITCHFINDER GENERAL

Manningtree is so small that there is only one patch of public grassland in the parish – the tiny Green, where some of Matthew Hopkins's victims were hanged. Hopkins was an unsuccessful Manningtree lawyer who came to prominence in 1645 and '46 in a region that was passionately anti-Catholic and pro-Royalist in the Civil War which had begun in 1642. Wandering preachers were urging the simple peasantry to denounce anything that stank of Catholicism and, by extension, of heresy and of witchcraft.

Hopkins saw his opportunity and denounced poor Elizabeth Clarke, a crippled woman from the village, but he was probably amazed when his interrogation drove Mrs Clarke to name 32 other women as fellow-witches. They were all taken to Chelmsford and hanged, but Hopkins had already recognised his new vocation and he proclaimed himself as the Witchfinder General, armed with the Devil's list of all English witches. ·

He set off with two assistants to rid the eastern counties of sorcerers, receiving £6 from Aldeburgh Corporation, £15 from King's Lynn, and £23 from Stowmarket, at a time when 1/6d (7½p) was the weekly wage for the average labourer.

Hopkins soon developed a near-infallible technique for sniffing out witches. The suspect woman was tied with the big toe of each foot to the thumb of the opposite hand and in this ignominious stance she was lowered by a rope around her waist into the nearest pond or river. If she sank she was innocent – but she had to drown to prove her innocence – and if she floated she was guilty, and was duly hanged.

Soon Hopkins began introducing other refinements into this otherwise uninteresting pastime; such as searching the victims' bodies for evidence of their having sold their souls to the Devil. Proof? This was in the form of any blemish on the skin. What other people saw as moles or birthmarks, Hopkins realised in his wisdom were the scars left when the Devil took his due. As Old Nick grew more astute, so did Hopkins, and soon any point on the skin which failed to produce blood when pricked with a sharp needle, was recognised as the Devil's mark.

Stage dagger. The Witchfinder General convicted several women of witchcraft by sticking a three-inch (7cm) spike into their buttocks without drawing blood or producing pain. What the spectators didn't know was that the spike's blade retracted into the handle as in a modern stage dagger.

Now you must understand, as Hopkins did, that the Devil gave each of his disciples on initiation one or more agents, which were usually disguised as harmless small animals. Many lonely old widows who in innocence had the audacity to keep a pet cat thus found themselves being tortured until they confessed that Tibbles was really Satan in disguise. One such victim, kept for three days and nights without sleep – plus a few other refinements – confessed that during this time she was visited by a kitten, two dogs, a rabbit, a toad and a polecat: what sane person could doubt her guilt? For good measure she confessed her other crimes, that she had slept with the Devil, and that his other agents were Jarama, a fat little dog with short legs, and Vinegar Tom, a greyhound. This particular confession forms an illustration in Hopkins's own book on how to sniff out sorceresses.

The Witchfinder General held the eastern counties in terror for 14 months until he retired to Manningtree in 1646, a wealthy man. Legend claims that he was later accused of being in league with the Devil and was hanged, but he probably died in 1647 of nothing worse than tuberculosis.

The Coggeshall fuller. Almost a century before Hopkins came onto the scene, Manningtree was recovering from another atrocity, the burning alive in 1555 of Thomas Osmond, a fuller from Coggeshall (a fuller cleaned freshly-woven woollen cloth and gave it a bulkier appearance). Osmond was convicted for the heinous crime of following his chosen religion and refusing to denounce it when so ordered. "He hath neglected to receive Mass at Easter, whereupon he was...condemned to the flames." His death, in the year that Bishop

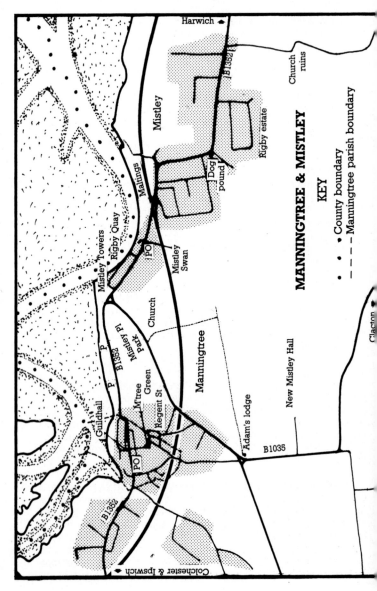

MANNINGTREE & MISTLEY

KEY

- • • County boundary
- – – – Manningtree parish boundary

Harwich →

B1352

Church ruins

Mistley

Rigby estate

Dog pound

Maltings

Rigby Quay

Mistley Towers

PO

Mistley Swan

Church

Manningtree

B1352

Mistley Pl Park

P

P

Guildhall

Mtree Green

Regent St

PO

P

B1352

Colchester & Ipswich →

Adam's lodge

New Mistley Hall

B1035

Clacton →

Latimer was burnt at the stake in Oxford, was intended as a warning, but instead it started a minor uprising which was subdued only by an assurance that the poor man's soul had gone to Heaven. In 1748 a plaque was put up in Manningtree church explaining this finer point; when the church was demolished the plaque was transferred to Mistley.

Bishop Bonner. Bishop Edmund Bonner was the man responsible for condeming Osmond to the stake. Bonner himself, a Catholic, was driven from office and was lucky to escape with his life; he died peacefully in 1569.

C Imond 2fonr

Bishop Edmund Bonner's signature.

Alston family. The Alston family, some of whom were buried in those lead-lined coffins, was among Manningtree's local aristocracy and owned the Great House in the High Street. This house, long since demolished to make way for the Post Office, provided shelter for the body of Queen Caroline of Brunswick on its journey from London to Harwich: the wife of George IV, she had died in 1821, and was on her way back home.

Packet Hotel. The Packet Hotel has also gone. This was not only the home of the local petty sessions but was also a hostelry that allowed its guests to go out by the back door, straight onto a packet steamer bound for Harwich. Townsend's stationery shop now occupies the site.

Corn Exchange. Among the buildings that have survived is the Corn Exchange, opened in 1865 but closed after only 10 years due to a recession in agriculture. Despite the Corn Law fiasco of 1815 which decreed that corn may not be imported until the price at home reached 80/- (£4) a quarter, this later collapse in the grain trade was a little surprising since barley was already important in Mistley's economy. With only minor alterations, the Corn Exchange took on its present role as Catholic Church, being administered from Ipswich.

What was a 'quarter'? In our antiquated system of measures, eight gallons of wheat made one bushel; eight bushels made one quarter; *five* quarters made one load, and two loads made one last.

'Great Towne.' Small though Manningtree may be, its history is large. Records of 1274 show the settlement under the name of *Manitre*, probably a corruption of 'many trees,' but there's no mention of the village in Domesday, the popular assumption being that it was then known as *Sciddenchow*, which was in reality the manor in the parish of Mistley.

In the reign of Edward VI, from 1547 to 1553, 'Manytre' was described very glowingly as *a Great Towne and also a Haven Towne, having in it the Nombre of seven hundrethe housling People* – double the modern population, and at a time when England had only around 5,000,000 people, housling or otherwise.

It had a *Key (Quay), crane, and common storehouse for the Receipte and Stowage of Goodes and Marchandise*, and the same authority said that *the inhabitants thereof are much employed in shippage and navigation and are a great Defense unto the Countrye adjoining*.

Some things have changed in 450 years. Manningtree's quay now serves nothing larger than pleasure craft, and many of today's inhabitants are much employed in Ipswich, Colchester and London.

Longest platform. A final touch. Rail commuters from Manningtree wait on what was the longest platform in England, until the title went to Colchester.

MANNINGTREE SHOPS. Manningtree is a small but vibrant shopping centre based around High Street and overflowing into South and North streets as well as into Lawford. The range of shops includes fashions, gifts, antiques, baker, florists, cycle & radio, shoes & leatherware, do it yourself, newsagent, delicatessen, art, jewellery, wools, books and stationery, wines, office supplies, hairdressers, butcher, children's clothes. **For eating:** Dragon House Chinese take-away; fish & chips; Indian Village take-away (in the old Guildhall); Stour Bay café. **Pubs:** The Crown, Red Lion, Swan, White Hart, and Skinner's Arms.

MISTLEY

The South Sea Bubble. The South Sea Company was formed in 1711 to clear a large debt by venturing into trade with Latin America, for which purpose it received a Government monopoly. When trading prospects failed to reach expectations the over-capitalised company offered to buy the National Debt of £31,000,000 for £7,500,000 cash.

The Government accepted the offer and straightway the fraudulent practises began. The directors of the South Sea Company managed to force up the nominal value of its stock from a listing of 130 in February 1720 to 1,050 in June of that year. The nation went wild on a gambling speculation, many people making fortunes overnight on the paper value of worthless shares – and when the notorious South Sea Bubble burst a few weeks later and that same stock plummeted in value to 135 by November, fortunes were lost equally fast.

Richard Rigby. The lucky, or the wily, were those who bought at the beginning and sold at the peak. Such a man was Richard Rigby, who already had a considerable fortune before the South Sea Company came on the money market, but his fortune after the burst was sufficient for him to begin putting into pracice the ideas he had long dreamed of: the development of Mistley into something special.

But let us backtrack a little. The Rigbys had come to the Stour estuary in 1703 when one Edward of that family, a London linen-draper, received the Mistley estates as part of the settlement of the affairs of the Earl of Oxford. Son Richard sold the linen business and so raised the funds to invest in the adventures of those South Sea merchants.

Richard now settled in Mistley, building for himself the first Mistley Hall, down what is now the cinder track leading from the main crossroads a little to the south of Manningtree. As a result of his will of 1730 the Rigby Charity came into existence and is still distributed each year by the parish council.

Castle Rising MP. But it was the second Richard Rigby who really spread himself with his grand ideas, and he had the money with which to do it. He started his Parliamentary career as one of the members for Castle Rising, a tiny village near King's Lynn which for generations returned two members to Parliament although it had fewer people than Manningtree. He graduated to being Member for Tavistock in Devon and, after saving the Duke of Bedford from attack, he was awarded the post of Paymaster General to the Forces of George III at the time of the American War of Independence, which was almost certainly the most lucrative post in the land. At any rate, he made £2,500,000 in 16 years.

Prince of Wales. On the home front he decided that Mistley was to become a spa, the place at which no young aristocrat dare *not* be seen, and in those halcyon days Mistley Hall was temporary home to Robert Walpole, the first Prime Minister and later the first Lord Orford. Also present were Garrick the dramatist and the Prince of Wales.

Rigby, still enjoying life as a 'Bedford' man, became lord of two manors in East Bergholt, commissioned Robert Adam in 1776 to design Mistley Church, the funds for which were provided in the first Richard Rigby's will, plus two lodges for the entrance to the drive to the Hall, which he also rebuilt extensively. One of those lodges remains, in a poor state of repair.

Rigby's expansionist ideas also took him to East Bergholt where he bought the lordship of two manors. Meanwhile, Adam also designed the **Swan Basin,** which still stands opposite the Mistley Thorn pub, and he drew plans for a saltwater bath, which never got off the ground, far less into it.

Mistley Towers. But the most impressive remains of all this activity are the twin Mistley Towers with their freestanding columns, the porticos built by Adam in 1776 for the church that had gone up in 1735. You'd like to look inside? The property is owned by English Heritage and entry is free; a notice on the fence names the holder of the keys.

Alas for dreams. The spa never materialised; Mistley Hall was demolished in 1844 when the estates were sold to pay gambling debts, and the nave of Mistley's second church was pulled down in 1870, leaving just the towers. The only evidence today that the Rigbys ever passed this way is in the names of Rigby Quay and Rigby, Avenue.

Acorn. The Mistley Hall which is marked on the Ordnance Survey maps is not to be confused with that of Rigby's era; it's a little to the south of the last remaining lodge to the former hall, and was sold in 1975 for conversion to a home for the mentally handicapped. Its name is Acorn, an acronym for *a community of real need*.

Mistley Railway. The adventure with Robert Adam was not the only local scheme to go wrong. The Mistley, Thorpe and Walton Railway also comes into this class since virtually all that is to be seen of the project today is the bridge which carries the B1352 Harwich road over where the line should have been.

Mistley was already comfortably sited on the branch line from Manningtree to Harwich and, some miles to the south, another line was going slowly eastwards from Colchester to Great Clackton – its arrival led to the creation of Clacton-on-Sea, without the 'k.' But in 1863 the Mistley, Thorpe and Walton Railway Company was incorporated; in 1864 the plans were amended for the line to end at Thorpe-le-Soken where it would meet the Clacton line, which had ideas for its own branch to Walton-on-the-Naze.

The first sod was cut on 6 April, 1864, but from the start things went badly. Delays and procrastination caused so many amendments to the schedule that the contractor was dismissed, but refused to quit the site until forcibly driven from it after losing a battle between 50 of his navvies and 60 longshoremen whom the company brought in from Harwich.

Money troubles. The MT&WR then ran into money troubles. In 1868 work ceased, and the next year the line was abandoned altogether and the company wound up. With it went the last hopes that there might also be a Manningtree to Bures line, via Dedham and Nayland.

Television. To strike a balance, Mistley does have one project that got off the ground – 447ft (136m) off, to be exact. On 22 May, 1962, the Manningtree television booster transmitter opened for the BBC. With its base 118ft (36m) above mean sea level, it means that the top of the mast, visible for many miles, is 565ft (172m) above the river level.

The programmes came to Manningtree by landline from the Aldeburgh booster station, which picked them up by direct transmission from the Tacolneston mast near Wymondham, Norfolk (Tacolneston is pronounced *Tackelston* and Wymondham is pronounced

Windam), but for years the mast has been transmitting BBC radio only; 1, 2, 3, 4, 5 and BBC Radio Essex.

Malt. Down by Mistley railway station another tall structure breaks the skyline. This is the chimney which carries the strange word EDME, the acronym for English Diastatic Malt Extracts. Edme and Allied Breweries, along with other companies, have dominated Mistley's economy, as well as its skyline, for generations; company names change as a result of take-overs and mergers, and in the late 1970s the entire process of making malt was automated.

But the old maltings remain. As you come down the hill from New Mistley and the Rigby Estate, those gaunt buildings on your right, blocking a splendid view of the Stour estuary, are the maltings, quarry-tiled floor upon floor with no headroom wasted.

Before automation, raw barley was tipped into large hoppers and soaked in water for about two days; then it was spread out on those floors an inch or so deep and continually turned, day and night, by men dragging large wooden rakes. After four or five days the barley grains had begun to germinate, at which point the entire load was poured into kilns and dried at temperatures ranging from 160°F to 215°F (71°C to 101°C), coming out for cleaning and storage as the finished malt. To the untrained eye and at a quick glance, there's no difference between barley and malt, but the discerning nose cannot be mistaken.

Mistley Quay Workshops. Come a little further down the hill and you find the Mistley Quay Workshops almost out of sight behind Adam's swan basin. In a building which for years was the sackmending shed for maltsters Brooks Savill, Ben Cooper opened his craft workshops in 1980 (✆0206.393884), and he now has an unusual selection of craftspeople including Anne and Ian Tucker who make harpsichords, Roger Davies who paints signs, Sara Paynter who works with Ben in the pottery, Con Rendall who makes and restores stringed instruments except harpsichords, Ruth Richmond who's involved with soft furnishings, and Graham Pearson who makes rigid furniture while Linda Owen and Carol Bowdrey run the tea shop. The workshops are open daily 100-1800, except the tea shop, closed Mon.

Haunted houses. Opposite, beside the post office, is the **Thorn Hotel,** (b&b a possibility), long known as the haunt of Old Harry who makes strange noises at night, walks through closed doors, and occasionally gets the blame for throwing small objects around. There are many stories of local hauntings: George used to wander around the **Red Lion** in Manningtree, several people claim to have seen a young woman in her wedding dress drift up from a grave in **Lawford** churchyard, and others swear they have seen the lights on in the church at dead of night during the wartime blackout, and heard a spectral choir at practise.

Hopping Bridge, a small affair 200m west of Mistley Towers, has a strange ghost story. Many people, over many years, have seen the ghost of a man in a cloak gliding or running along the grass verge or across the road, usually at dusk or after dark, but always vanishing like the mists of morn by the bridge; this apparition has even been reported to the police. One witness went back to the spot in full daylight and swears there's a patch of grass about 6ft by 3ft (2m x 1m) that's greener than all the rest. Could there be a body buried beneath the sod?

Black Shuck. You've heard of Black Shuck, of course? You *haven't?* Shuck is a black dog, eyes as big as saucers, who roams East Anglian byways by night. His name comes from *scucca*, Anglo-Saxon for 'demon,' and he's as old as history. The Essex Shuck sometimes protects lonely travellers at night, but in Suffolk he may attack if challenged, and death usually follows. In Norfolk, stay well clear of Black Shuck, for nobody who sees him has long to live. He is a fearsome herald of death, if not its carrier.

Mistley Church. But back to brighter things. Continue west from the Thorn, turn left at Mistley Towers, and Mistley's third Church of St Mary is on your left, built in 1870-'71 in Gothic Revival style and one of the few churches in East Anglia to have a tall spire: this one reaches to 140ft (42.5m) and uses stone shipped in from Caen, Normandy. The ornately-carved organ case came from Worcester Cathedral, and another prime feature is the window showing the Last Judgement.

The church is too new to have brasses, but it has brought over from Manningtree's church the plaques which tell the story of **Thomas Tusser,** (see Brantham) and of Thomas Osmond, who was burned at Manningtree. Also here is Manningtree's silver communion plate, presented by Archbishop Laud of Canterbury, owner of the land on which Manningtree church was built.

Archbishop Laud. William Laud was born at Reading in 1573 and became Archbishop of Canterbury in 1633. He was anti-Catholic, but as he was also anti-Puritan the Long Parliament charged him with high treason in December 1640; he went for trial in March 1644 and was executed at Tower Hill on 10 January 1645. And only a few months later, Matthew Hopkins began his reign of terror.

Mistley Church is usually locked; the key is available from the rectory in Stour St, Manningtree. And Mistley's previous churches? The second was, of course, at the nearby towers, and the first was on the eastern edge of the parish; its remains are still there, beside the scar of the failed MT&W Railway.

Mistley Place Park. Roughly opposite the present church is Mistley Place Park, a 27-acre (11ha) reserve for animals saved from slaughter or neglect. Owned by Peter and Michael Taylor, the park is open daily 0900 to dusk for £1 (pensioners and children 50p), *dogs not admitted.* Many varieties of domestic poultry and geese live in harmony with wild duck and swans, and among the rescued livestock you can see Soay sheep which originated on that island south of Skye. The grounds have some good woodland, including a Californian redwood tree, and a lake with a small island.

There's a tea-shop in the park, and a small play area for children.

Swans. Mistley's name means 'the pasture where the mistel (mistletoe) grows,' and was recorded in 1225 as *Misteleg* from its Domesday version of *Mitteslea,* but the village has been known for its swans for generations before Adam built that giant bird opposite the Thorn. Indeed, until the automation of several riverside mills and maltings, Mistley had the country's second largest flock of mute swans – the largest was, and is, at Abbotsbury in Dorset. The mutes are here the year round, joined in winter by the rare whooper or bewick and still supplementing their natural food from whatever they can find in the spillage from the maltings. You'll see them by Mistley Walls, west of the Towers, and also along Rigby Quay. A smaller flock tries to survive in the inner dock at Ipswich but has too much oil spillage and other pollution for comfort.

Other wildlife. The Stour's low-tide mudflats are feeding grounds to many wading birds, with rare sightings reported of spoonbill, bittern and red-necked phalarope; local photographer Charles Rose, who has shown his work on television, recalled a brave oystercatcher which nested between the tracks of the main-line railway near Cattawade years ago. It stood on guard beside the track every time a train went over its nest.

If you know where to look you can find fallow deer and badger in the Stour valley, and maybe an otter in the upper reaches beyond Sudbury.

Wildfowling. Inevitably, mankind harvested the crop of wildlife through the ages, with Mistley men evolving their own version of the wildfowlers' punt, 16ft to 18ft long and 3ft in the beam (4.8m to 5.5m by 0.9m wide), and drawing a mere 2in (5cm) with a freeboard of 10in (25cm). Built of timber, this craft was propelled by two 6ft (2m) oars to the fishing and fowling grounds and provided the only source of income to several families in bygone years. In recent times with wildfowling by punt a thing of the past and windsurfing yet to come, the local sailing club organised spectacular races between punts fitted with Bermuda-rig sails.

Shipbuilding. In Mistley, several family names have been linked with tidewater activities for generations, and as late as the 1930s the quays at Mistley and Manningtree were lined with motor and sailing craft from British and continental ports, and the last of those barges that plied upstream to Sudbury. The first great family was Rigby

Mistley's nineteenth-cent church is in Gothic Revival style.

which gave the village its quay, and it was a Rigby who built the first ship to be launched here, in 1770. The shipyard, a little to the east of the Mistley Quay Workshops, produced many vessels including a 300-ton West Indiaman, and 12 men-of-war of which the largest was the 914-ton 32-gun *Amphian*, which was Nelson's flagship for a time.

His name is Mudd. During the 19th cent the Howards and the Tovells owned the yard, building fishing cutters. The Howards had more than 20 cutters, the largest fleet of its kind on the East Coast between the Humber and London. But in 1852 the railway company urged the Howards to leave Mistley for Hull, tempted by the offer of free rail transport to London for all its catches. Aboard one of the vessels was Harrison Mudd and his family. Mudd prospered at Hull, became skipper, built up his own fleet, and even today the name of Mudd is known throughout the fishing industry.

Large-scale commercial fishing finished with the Howards, and shipbuilding itself finished in the 1860s, but in 1920 one F.W. Horlock began building again, this time at the eastern end of the quay. Horlock built several steamers and six steel-hulled spritsail barges, the last of which, the *Blue Mermaid,* was also the last of its type to be built in Britain.

Thames barge. The spritsail barge, more popularly known as the Thames barge, was developed especially for the shallow estuaries of the East Coast, its flat bottom augmented by retractable lee-boards; it was a larger version of the Norfolk wherry, and carried more than

2,000sq ft (200sq m) of canvas, which one man and a boy could handle.

The barges ceased trading shortly after World War Two, but many have been restored, usually at great cost, and some of the 30 seaworthy craft still put in at Mistley Quay for a courtesy visit.

Dog pound. You'd like to see something unusual? Where the road bends sharp left in New Mistley, stands a sycamore tree surrounded by a brick wall topped by a fence. Why wall up a tree? The truth is, the wall and fence are an ancient dog pound, and the sycamore just happens to be growing there. And across the fields to the south you may see an aerial. Don't tell anybody, but this marks the site of a nuclear fallout shelter.

MISTLEY SHOPS. Mistley is dominated by its much smaller neighbour, Manningtree, and has a small post office and stores by the swan basin. Up the hill in New Mistley are two general stores, a butcher and a fish-and-chip shop. **Pub:** The Anchor.

LAWFORD

Lawford is a village that has lost its ancient centre. In the north-east it merges with Manningtree near where the old ironworks of Offwood Bendall, Esq, once stood. At the south-west, the flat, fertile lands worked by tenants of the now-defunct **Land Settlement Association** at the Foxash Estate, merge into Ardleigh.

Between these extremes lie the big new housing estates and the small old estates while, due to the disappearance of the medieval village centre, the church, the manors, the pubs and the village hall now stand in fairly open country.

Shirburn. To the north-west, on the 'shire' boundary with Colchester Borough Council and overshadowed by the railway embankment, stands the 'shire burn' or Shirburn Mill, believed to be the only overshot water-mill in Essex, beside the site of two other mills – one Saxon, one Norman – mentioned in Domesday. The present timber building dates from around 1820-'30 and had a wooden wheel, later replaced by a metal one 18ft (5.5m) in diameter and weighing many tons. It was in working order until 1937, drawing its power from two millponds, but during World War Two the wheel went for scrap for munitions.

Shir Burn. The stream, the Shir Burn, is fed by a cluster of springs along the tiny valley, and the water from one known as Almonds Well was barrelled and freighted to London as an eye lotion when the railway opened in 1846.

Margaret Thatcher. The village hall, Ogilvie Hall, is a memorial to the family which used to live in the nearby **Lawford Place,** which more recently was a research laboratory for Bakelite Xylonite, the plastics manufacturer on the estuary (see Brantham). The Ogilvies are somewhat overshadowed by a research chemist who worked here for a while before going into politics and becoming the longest-serving Prime Minister of this century. By the way, Margaret Thatcher has a married sister living at Little Oakley, near Harwich.

Manors. The two manors of Lawford are Dale Hall, in the new housing estate, and Lawford Hall, one time home of Edward Waldegrave, who built it in 1583; another Edward Waldegrave is remembered in Borley Church. Apart from leaving his name on the council estate this lord of the manor was not too distantly related to Catherine Howard, fifth wife of Henry VIII; his wife, Joan Ackworth, was private secretary to the queen. A descendant of the Waldegrave family gave Lawford Hall its Georgian appearance in 1756, and a later descendant was a cabinet minister in Mrs Thatcher's government.

Church. The chancel of St Mary the Virgin's Church, which dates from 1340, is one of the best examples of Gothic work in Essex, but the damage to the chancel carvings was almost certainly done in the 17th cent by Cromwell's men. There is a memorial to the 19th-cent Dean Merivale who rowed in the first Oxford and Cambridge boat race and went on to write the history of the Roman Empire. The tower is a colourful mix of brick, dressed and rough stone, and flint, looking as if it has been patched many times.

LAWFORD SHOPS. Co–op supermarket and smaller shops by the end of Manningtree High Street. **Pubs:** in upper Lawford, King's Arms; in lower Lawford, Skinner's Arms.

BRANTHAM

The first field of barley to be grown in the eastern counties was seeded at Brantham, on the field now crossed by the A137 as it heads north into Suffolk from the Cattawade barrage. It's not known whether this crop was to supply some early malting needs of Mistley but it's more likely that Mistley's industry grew from this enterprise at Brantham.

Thomas Tusser. Thomas Tusser, the poet farmer of Braham Hall – note the spelling – was the 16th cent innovator, and he made certain the event was recorded for posterity by putting it in his classic textbook *A Hundred Pointes of Good Husbandrie.*

> In Brantham, where rie but no barlie did growe,
> good barlie I had, as meany did knowe;
> Five seame of an aker I truely was paid,
> for thirtie lode muck of each aker so laid.

Few farmers today could find 30 loads of muck for an acre of grain, and there's the pity of it. But what soil is best for growing this new grain? Tusser wrote:

Some of Mistley's swans feeding on the maltings' outflow.

> As grauell and sand is for rie and not wheat,
> (or yeeldeth hir burden to tone the more great,)
> So peason [peas] and barlie delight not in sand,
> but rather in claie or in rottener land.

Tusser wrote his treatise while living at Braham Hall, the farm that lies on the uphill side of the region's first barley field. Publishing his effort in 1557 he then moved to Poultry, London, where in nostalgia for the open country – although Poultry was still not far from green fields – he added to the original in 1573 and '77, culminating in the massive *Fiue Hundred Pointes...* The complete work was republished by the English Dialect Society in 1878, faithfully reproducing the original spelling, as I have done, and this reprint insists that only the first hundred 'pointes' were compiled at Brantham, which belies Tusser's memorial in Mistley Church.

It is difficult for us today to recapture the feeling of the peasant's life of four centuries ago, but Tusser gives a revealing picture when he recommends the ploughman's menu:

> Good ploughmen looke weekly, of custome and right,
> for roast meat on Sundaies and Thursdaies at night.
> This doing and keeping such custom and guise,
> they call thee good huswife, they loue thee likewise.

Month by month, the husbandman was told what jobs he should be doing, and what symptoms to look for in his beasts – in fact, farming life in those days could be lived according to the Creed of Tusser, and in recognition of this the Essex Agricultural College at Writtle, Chelmsford, takes as a motto the opening line of Tusser's work:

Time tries the truth, in euerie thing.

But what beef farmer today would contravene the law by becoming his own vet and adopting this method of making sure a bullock doesn't lose 'her' teeth:

Poor bullock, with browsing and naughtily fed,
scarce feedth, hir teeth be so loose in hir hed:
Then slise ye the taile where ye feele it so soft,
with soote and with garlick bound it to aloft.

Braham Hall. But the Braham Hall (pronounce it to rhyme with *calm*) of Tusser's time is not the building that stands there today, although there are still some very old parts; nor is it the building that is mentioned in Domesday – which tells us in passing that Brantham was a league long and half a league broad, and paid 18d (7.5p) in gelt (money).

Burned Community. Ekwall suggests in his *Dictionary of English Placenames* that Brantham was Brant's ham, Brant's community, but since Brentwood in Essex is derived from the German *brannt*, 'burned,' and it is known that Olaf Tryggvason the Dane visited our

The Swan Basin at Mistley with the Quay Workshops behind.

little community in 991 and burned it to the ground, 'burned community' would seem a more logical derivation.

Domesday. After the Norman Conquest and the resultant Domesday survey, Brantham moved into recorded history, and was already overshadowed by the nearby Bercold, where the defeated King Harold had had his principal lordship, an offshoot of the **Lawford Hall** which he also held. Yet Brantham Church was soon to be more important, and East Bergholt's house of prayer was relegated to the role of lady chapel, which will have some bearing on why the present church there is still unfinished.

The third incumbent at Brantham, who also ministered to the chapel at Bercold, held his living by the patronage of the Abbot of Battle, who had also sponsored the livings at Mistley, and at Bentley in Suffolk. This patronage at Brantham was far from a fleeting thing as the abbot and convent appointed 20 of the next 23 priests, until the mid-16th cent and the Reformation.

St Michael. The Church of St Michael the Archangel which is at the top of the modern village, replaces a timber building dating from around 1277, the flint for this new church having come from a quarry by the estuary near where recent excavations have exposed traces of that original settlement burned by the Danes 1,000 years ago.

Constable painting. Constable gave large a painting of *Christ Blessing the Children* to the church, where it hung until the 1980s when the threat of theft or vandalism became too great. The picture went first to Christchurch Mansion in Ipswich but may move to Emmanuel College, Cambridge, which holds the patronage of Brantham Church.

An insurance quotation in 1927 valued the work at £500 but today it would be worth a fortune, despite an earlier rector having removed Constable's signature (he also chipped masons' names from the gravestones), and a baby at the breast having been overpainted in Victorian times. Lady Owen Mackenzie of the National Gallery commented on "...figure subjects by Constable being so rare. This is not surprising for obviously his ability for that style of work was far inferior to that of landscape."

Plastics factories. No visitor to Brantham can fail to see the factories which sit on the Stour estuary on the southern bounds of the village. Together these are the largest employers in the entire Stour valley, drawing in workers from the neighbouring towns.

The first factory you reach down the narrow lane is **Wardle Storey,** successor to the Bakelite Xylonite company which set up here in 1887 to produce celluloid. The factory makes many types of plastic sheet and film on its 90-acre site, including the only synthetic camphor made in Britain – and the UK production of table tennis balls depends on celluloid (xylonite) made on machinery that has survived from the beginning of the century. The company also turns out thermoplastics sheeting in a wide range, which is used in many products from cars to jet aircraft. In 1940 BX was one of the first in the world to make sheet and tube from PVC, and this is still an important part of the factory's business.

The second large factory is **ICI Imagedata,** known until 1990 as Bexford. Founded just after World War Two by a group of dedicated technicians, it became the world's largest independent maker of photographic film base. Another superlative: the factory had some of the world's largest casting machines to meet the demand for high quality at low cost.

It's doubtful if Tusser would have approved.

> Where plastics ye make on factorie site,
> the barlie neuer groweth, a true sorrie plight.

BRANTHAM SHOPS. Brantham comes under Manningtree's influence, and in the lower village, called 'New Village' because it was built for BX's workers, is a post office and a fish-and-chip shop. The true new village, at the top of the hill, has a Spar grocer, a newsagent and one other shop.

Pubs: The Bucks by the riverside has a good restaurant, and other pubs are the Ark and the Crown, all in the *old* New Village. The charming Bull Inn is beyond the railway bridge.

BRADFIELD

Bradfield is a small village to the east of Mistley, but with a strange claim to historic fame. Sir Harbottle Grimston, the second baronet, lived at Bradfield Hall during Matthew Hopkins's reign of terror in Manningtree. The Grimston family had come from Suffolk and had legal traditions; Sir Harbottle, a Puritan though not an extremist in his views, was Member of Parliament for Harwich from 1628, and after the restoration of the monarchy in 1660 he became Speaker of the House and Master of the Rolls, but in Bradfield he is better known for having tried the judges who tried Charles I and sentenced him to death; he also tried some of the judges who sent the Witchfinder General's victims to the gallows.

Bradfield's Church of St Lawrence is mainly 13th cent, but the tower is 16th cent and looks like a patchwork quilt. Inside, as well as memorials to the Grimstons, there is one to Squadron Commander Edwin Harris Dunning of the Royal Flying Corps, the first officer to land an aircraft successfully on the deck of a ship under way. The ship was *HMS Furious* and the date was 2 August, 1917.

BRADFIELD SHOPS. Post Office stores. **Pubs:** Ram and Hoggett, Village maid, Strangers Home.

3: CONSTABLE'S COUNTRY

Flatford to Stratford

JOHN CONSTABLE WAS BORN at **East Bergholt** on 11 June, 1776, the second son and fourth child of Golding Constable, the local miller, and his wife Anne.

Constable senior had moved his young family from Flatford Mill two years earlier into East Bergholt House, a new, solid, red-brick building near the centre of the village, in anticipation of more babies arriving. John was the first of the family's children to be born here.

At first, Golding Constable hoped his second son would become a clergyman, but later he wanted John to follow him into the profitable milling business. John had wanted to be a painter from childhood and had no aptitude for milling or other business although he gave it a year's trial to satisfy his father. The young Constable soon befriended John Dunthorne, the plumber, glazier, simple artist and village atheist whose shop was at the street end of the short drive to the Constable family home. The friendship showed the village where John's thought lay, but the alliance with an atheist displeased the village rector, who was eventually to be Constable's relation by marriage.

Moss Cottage. Constable later rented Moss Cottage, a tiny house now part of a motor mechanic's workshop by the post office; later still, he bought it and the neighbouring house.

Constable's mother introduced John to Sir George Beaumont, the art connoisseur and amateur painter who had made a fortune in mining coal; his mother lived in Dedham. Mrs Constable probably thought Sir George would dissuade her son, but Sir George offered practical advice, encouragement, and eventually persuaded the miller to give his son a small allowance and let him go to the Royal Academy Schools in London. Sir George was later a founder benefactor of the National Gallery.

Maria Bicknell. Constable started his studies in 1799, aged 23, and exhibited his first work at the academy in 1802. He often went home to East Bergholt and on one of his visits he met the girl who was to become his wife, then the 12-year-old Maria Bicknell, grand-daughter of the irritable rector, Dr Rhudde.

Constable continued with his studies. He went to the Lake District in 1806 and did the Borrowdale series of water colours now at the Victoria and Albert Museum; he painted *Malvern Hall, Warwick*, (Tate Gallery) in 1808, but he often went home to East Bergholt. Gradually his friendship with Maria turned to love, and his relationship with Dr Rhudde consequently turned to animosity. The rector was happy with the Constables as parishioners, but he stubbornly opposed the idea of his grand-daughter marrying a member of the gentry who had taken a step down the social ladder and who could scarcely make a living. Finally, in October 1816 when Maria was 21 and John 32, the couple defied family opinions and married at St Martin's-in-the-Fields

Happy marriage. The couple had chosen wisely; the marriage was happy though for years there was seldom any cash to spare. John was painting, but he had chosen to be a landscape artist at a time when fashion demanded portraits, with the result that he had not achieved the recognition that he wanted, and which was essential for him to command a high enough price for his work.

Among his earlier pictures are *Boatbuilding near Flatford Mill*, in 1814, *Golding Constable's Kitchen Garden* in 1815 (Christchurch Museum, Ipswich, with others), *Elm Trees in Old Hall Park*, in 1817, and the *View of Dedham from Old Hall*, painted at the request of Thomas Fitzhugh, husband-to-be of Elizabeth Godfrey of the hall. Maria, meanwhile, had begun to produce her seven babies.

Recognition. Then came 1819, when Constable painted *The White Horse* (Frick Collection, New York), his largest canvas so far and his first work to win acclaim. While the White Horse was on display at the Royal Academy, Dr Rhudde died, leaving £4,000 to Maria; this, added to John's share of the proceeds of his family home from the recent death of his parents, gave the Constable family financial security for the first time. The White Horse also influenced Constable's fellow artists who at last elected him as an Associate of the Royal Academy.

With recognition slowly coming, Constable still kept his links with East Bergholt and came back to the village on many occasions from his rented home in Hampstead or Brighton. He said of the Suffolk-Essex countryside: "Those scenes made me a painter, and I am grateful. I had often thought of pictures before ever I had touched a pencil."

Remembering his fellow-artist Thomas Gainsborough who died in 1788, Constable praised Suffolk in particular: "It is a most delightful landscape for a painter. I fancy I see Gainsborough in every hedge and hollow tree. The landscape of Gainsborough is soothing, tender and affecting."

Hay Wain. He painted the *Hay Wain* (National Gallery) in 1821, now his most famous work and certainly among the most popular pre-Impressionist paintings to come from a British artist, but it stirred no interest in England at the time; its original title of *Landsacape – Noon*, didn't help. The following April a Parisian dealer named Arrowsmith offered him £70, but Constable refused to sell for less than £150 although he needed the money. Later, Arrowsmith bought *The Hay Wain*, *View on the Stour by Dedham*, and a Yarmouth seascape, for £250.

In 1823 came *Salisbury Cathedral from Bishop's Grounds*, then in 1824 Arrowsmith exhibited his three Constables at the Paris Salon and created a sensation which prompted Charles X of France to award Constable a gold medal.

Recognition in Britain was still slow to come. There followed *The Leaping Horse* and *Summer Afternoon After a Shower* in 1825, *The Cornfield* in 1826, *The Glebe Farm* and *Hampstead Heath* in 1827, and in 1828 *Dedham Vale* and *Stream Bordered With Willows*, the latter rejected by the Royal Academy's hanging committee.

1828 was a bad year. Maria had been suffering from the family ailment of tuberculosis for years, and in November she died.

Constable, R.A. The next year the RA elected Constable to full membership of the academy, the ultimate accolade but desperately overdue. Constable applied himself to his work and produced, among others, *The Opening of Waterloo Bridge* in 1832, *Salisbury Cathedral From The Meadows* in 1834 and *The Valley Farm* in 1835. He died suddenly in London on 31 March, 1837, supposedly from indigestion, and is buried in Hampstead Cemetery.

Anonymity lives on. Despite his later fame as England's leading landscape artist – you may disagree if you are a Turner supporter – East Bergholt *still* has done little to commemorate its local lad. The only official indication is a tiny section of stained glass in one window of the parish church, and a recently-added notice marking the site of East Bergholt House, Constable's birthplace. The house was demolished in the 1840s because the owner of the house opposite, West Lodge, claimed it spoiled his view.

More information on the artist is in *John Constable*, by Freda Constable, Lavenham Press, 1975.

Constable's Country. Legend claims that the name of this part of the Stour valley, Constable's Country, came from a conversation the artist overheard in the stagecoach as he was nearing home. A woman passenger admiring the landscape, asked her companion where they were. "Constable's Country" was the reply. Constable never revealed his identity to them, but he told the story in London and so the name stuck.

EAST BERGHOLT and Flatford

There is no way in which East Bergholt can be considered a typical English village. For a start, the Constable connection brings tourists from all over the country, from the continent, and from English-speaking lands oceans away.

Stockbroker belt. Apart from that, the village has more retired gentry, ex-Army officers and commuting City tycoons than you would expect to find in a moderate-sized town. But it's all at low key and you must live in the village or, as I did, be a local newspaper reporter, to make the contacts. Take a careful look through *Debrett's Peerage* and *Who's Who* to see what I mean.

Apart from John Constable, the best-known local resident was the late **Randolph Churchill,** son of the wartime Prime Minister, who lived in what was West Lodge (see above), later to be known simply and impressively as Stour, but now called Stour House. **Edward Ardizzoni** the cartoonist, official war artist 1940-'46, and illustrator of more than 170 books, was born in Haiphong, Vietnam, in 1900, but spent his childhood in the house called Gothics, with his mother and sister. His memoirs recall his first impressions on going into the convent (now Old Hall, see later) from which the nun Madge Moult escaped, and wondering if he would ever get out alive. **Paul Jennings,** Sunday newspaper journalist and author, lived for years near Dr Rhudde's rectory. The **Eley** family, whose name has been stamped on millions of cartridges, still owns property in the village. Old Hall is home to a BBC producer, and I know of other people with titles and high ranks who would rather keep their anonymity.

East Bergholt church: the tower would have been on the left.

Wool town. East Bergholt – West Bergholt is a suburb of Colchester – was mentioned in the Domesday records as Bercold, but it rose to prominence, like so many other villages, with the wool trade of the late 12th to the late 16th centuries. Wool was England's major export commodity for generations, the trade originally based in East Anglia and bringing wealth to dozens of small towns; the Industrial Revolution took the business to Bradford, Yorkshire, where the first wool-weaving mill opened in 1798.

Wool has given the English language so many words and phrases down the ages: *to be on tenterhooks* would have been painful as these hooks were used for stretching the finished cloth. The shape of the stretching rack has also given us the word *tent.* Go *woolgathering* and you wander aimlessly; originally you would have been gathering wool from random bushes. The *Woolsack* in the House of Lords is a reminder of the revenue that wool brought to the monarchy, and later governments have *fleeced* the population by over-taxation.

Think of our family names that derive from the wool trade: Carder, Dyer, Fuller, Lamb, Shepherd, Spinner, Taylor, Weaver. Look at pub signs all over the Eastern Counties for more reminders; in Suffolk alone there are *The Ram* at Hadleigh, *The Shoulder of Mutton* at Assington and Old Newton, *The Fleece* at Beccles, Groton and Mendlesham, *The Plough and Fleece* near Bradfield Combust, *The Bell and Steelyard* at Woodbridge – a steelyard was a device for weighing wool going for export – *The Shepherd and Dog* at Bury St Edmunds and near Stowmarket, and *The Woolpack* at Ipswich, Debenham, Haverhill and Fornham St Martin.

And which breed of sheep created all this wealth? The Norfolk horned, ironically now an endangered species, having been displaced in the 19th cent by the black-faced Suffolk.

East Bergholt was not among the greatest of the wool towns, but wool built Ardizzoni's Gothics, and Gables near the village pharmacy, as well as helping to finance the church. The village had evolved as a cluster of separate communities on a ring road around a huge expanse of common land – fenced and ploughed after the 1817 Enclosure Act – and the decline of the wool trade brought poverty to all; in 1734 a visitor wrote "The town is greatly reduced, many houses having lately been pulled down."

The village also lost its green – Churchill's Stour stands on the site – and with the death of the wool trade came the death of East Bergholt's market, held on land opposite Stour House and on Church Plain opposite Old Hall and the tourist office.

Another victim of the decline was the Lambe School, built in 1594 by Edward Lambe, lord of one of the four manors, and restored in 1974 as the village hall.

Peasants' Revolt. Apart from the wool trade's ups and downs, East

Bergholt played its small role in England's history. In 1381 the Peasants' Revolt, led by Wat Tyler and centred on Norwich, prompted a public rising in this village on 17 June, when a band of men led by Thomas Fletcher ordered William atte Heath, the bailiff of the Manor of Old Hall, to surrender the court rolls and property titles, which the mob then burned outside the church, showing its determination to be rid of serfdom; the crowd then surged off to **Stratford St Mary** and held the parson to ransom, getting 26/6d (£1.32½p) for him. The Bergholt bailiff chose to pay a fine rather than renew his appointment.

Protestant Revolt. Bergholt was in the news again in 1553 when Mary, daughter of Henry VIII and Catherine of Aragon, came to the throne amid widespread revolts between Protestant and Catholic. The next year Mary married Philip of Spain, who declared himself King of England, and Parliament voted to reunite with Rome. The new Church of England was having a hard time.

In East Bergholt, clergyman Robert Samuell was denounced and taken to Ipswich to be burned at the stake for his Protestant views. And in 1644, at the height of the Civil War, the Puritans of the village declared their rector to be 'malignant' and replaced him. This eventually led to the granting of a licence for Bergholt to have a dissenters' chapel, one of the first in the area, from which grew the Congregational Church; the present church, in Cemetery Lane, was built in 1856-'57 for £913.

When building ceased on East Bergholt's church tower, the bells were housed temporarily in this bellcage.

Then there was the strange case of John Mattinson, 'eleven years the beloved schoolmaster of this town' who was 'unfortunately shott' at the age of 32. His memorial in the church gives no details but comments that he was 'a terror and a delight' to his pupils.

St Mary's Church. The parish church of St Mary tells not only about Mattinson, and holds a monument to Edward Lambe, but it boasts the village's only true memorial to its most famous son in a small text at the bottom of the first stained glass window on the right, once you're in the nave. This says simply that *John Constable, R.A, born in this parish 1776, died 1857.* And on the roof of the south aisle, not accessible to tourists, this inscription is stamped into the lead: *T. Woodgate, J. Lott, churchwardens, 1811.* J. Lott, of course, was a descendant of the Willy Lott whose cottage features in Constable's *Hay Wain.*

Bellcage. East Bergholt's church is unusual in that it has neither tower nor steeple; it has a peal of bells, but nowhere in the church to hang them. One explanation is that a wealthy man living nearby in the mid-16th cent – the church dates from the mid-14th cent – didn't want to be disturbed by the ringing and so bribed everybody concerned not to complete the tower. More credible is the story which tells of ill-luck following the building of the tower which rises little more than half way to the nave roof and is topped off as if the masons are coming back after the winter. Despite numerous attempts, goes the tale, work could not proceed, and when a man was killed on the construction, all labour stopped permanently. Of course, *both* stories could be true?

The church's own version sounds even better. Cardinal Wolsey of Ipswich, who was personally financing the tower, had paid for only five years' of work at his death in November 1530. It is a fact that in 1531 the church authorities built a bellcage in the churchyard, to hold the bells temporarily – and they are still there.

Or do you like the final explanation? This claims that the Devil came along each night and undid the work of the previous day. But if this were true, wouldn't you find masonry scattered around the village?

Bells. The bells are rung every Sunday, 0930-1000 and (in summer only) 1800-1830. They are the only bells in England to be rung by swinging their headstocks.

Erratic. There *is* a large stone in a hedgerow to the east of the village (see map) but it's not the work of the Devil. It's a glacial erratic, a 200,000,000-year-old boulder brought down from Scotland or Scandinavia during the last Ice Age and standing where nature left it, England's southernmost evidence of glaciation until a similar stone was found in Harwich Harbour in 1974.

Gardens to visit. Near this erratic is **East Bergholt Place,** whose 17.5 acres (7ha) of gardens were laid out with ornamental and flowering trees by Charles Eley, whose family made the well-known ammunition until it sold out to ICI. The gardens have spectacular yew arches, examples of topiary, a 'coffee bean' tree, a palm, numerous azaleas, rhododendrons and magnolias and my favourite, a 'handkerchief tree' which blossoms in May. The gardens are **open** on the last Sunday in April and thereafter for the next three alternate Sundays, 1400-1800. Entry is £1 for adults, 25p for children, with all proceeds going to charity.

Another garden open to the public is that of Capt Christopher and Lady Anne Wake-Walker at **East Bergholt Lodge,** near the A12. Open days are random, or by appointment, and you'll need to ask in the village for details. The gardens cover about 10 acres (4ha) and hold around 140 varieties of rose, but there are also 200 acres (40ha) of woods. Admission is £1.

The National Gardens Scheme lists two other East Bergholt gardens which usually open 1400-1800 on the same June Sunday; **Rosemary,** on Rectory Hill, showing lawns, a lake and water garden, and specialising in azaleas and roses; the gardens extend to 8 acres (4ha). The other is **Stour Cottage,** in The Street (see the village map).

The 12 acres (5ha) of gardens at neighbouring **Stour House,** owned by Mr and Mrs Robert Wallace, are occasionally open, showing beautiful lawns, azaleas, mature woodland, rhododendrons and heathers, as well as a splendid view across the valley to Dedham church. Ask locally for dates.

Sir Alfred Munnings designed this picturesque bridge at Flatford.

OLD HALL

Old Hall, one of the original four manors of East Bergholt and the subject of several paintings by Constable, has probably the most unusual story of any building in the village.

The first records go back to 1290 when Bercold, formerly the royal manor of King Harold, had been divided into four: Old Hall, Illaries, Spencers, and St John's, the latter also known as Commandree.

Commandaria St John. But let us divert for a second. Henry II (1154-'89) had granted the manor of St John's to the Knights Templar, also known as the Knights of the Order of St John of Jerusalem, from where it took its name. The Templars had helped recapture the Holy Land and had seen Richard I, on the Third Crusade, briefly capture Cyprus. Richard sold Cyprus to the Knights who soon sold it again and moved on to Rhodes. But they left a military presence in Cyprus at Kolossi Castle, near Limassol, which they called the Commandaria St John. By the 14th cent the Commandaria had started to make wine, not surprisingly called Commandaria St John, which is still in production on the island and is claimed to be the world's oldest surviving vintage. The Templars' close relatives, the Knights Hospitaller, moved west from the Holy Land and took control of Malta in 1530 where in 1565 they survived an overpowering siege laid by Süleiman the Magnificent, built the world's only capital city to be named from its founder – Valletta – and then faded into obscurity, surviving as the modern St John Ambulance Brigade. A fuller account of the Templars' and Hospitallers' story is in *Discover Cyprus* and *Discover Malta* in this series.

Peasants' Revolt. Back to Old Hall. Under the English feudal system – the Scottish *udal* system was different – the lord of the manor was a local despot who ruled his villeins, the almost slavelike serfs, and his freemen, who had a little amount of personal choice. Villeins were obliged to work unpaid for their lord several times a year, notably at harvest, haymaking, and ploughing. The Peasants' Revolt of 1381, when bailiff William atte Heath was obliged to hand over the manorial rolls, was an abortive attempt to end feudalism, but Lady Margaret de Sutton and her husband John stayed at Old Hall.

In the early 15th cent Dame Elizabeth Howard, the Suttons' heir, married John de Vere, 12th Earl of Oxford, whose home was at **Castle Hedingham** in Essex, so for the next 150 years Old Hall had a succession of tenants. The steward fulfilled the duties of lord of the manor, and a record of 1423 gives the lord's expenses for a routine visit *for 3 days and 3 nights and for the charge of his horse and for parchment for writing this roll, 4s 7½d* (23p).

Records also show innumerable fines the peasants incurred for poaching on the ground of an absentee landlord, and recall sawpits (pits where sawyers cut up tree trunks) in the village street and pigs digging up the village green.

The 16th earl sold Old Hall to the Derehaugh family of Orford who had links with the Cardynalls of Great Bromley, south of Mistley. Both families tried to restore order in East Bergholt, the rolls recording their efforts: *Robert Knoppe est a brawler et quod Franciscus Bryant et Joh Abbott sunt drunckerdes.*

Town Meeters. By the late 16th cent the manorial courts were losing their power to parish assemblies, but Bergholt had in addition a self-elected body of *chiefest* (richest) inhabitants who called themselves the Town Meeters and who gave money to the parish poor but sent other paupers back to their native parish. We have an example of this early parish relief when Dr White was paid £5 *for laying Goody Wiard in bed.*

The last Cardynall died at the Battle of Edgehill in 1642, and in 1701 there is a record of Old Hall passing once more through female descent to Mercy Parker, who married 56-year-old Joseph Chaplin – there's a Chaplin's Road in the modern village – a self-made man who, with a little help from Queen Anne, had become High Sheriff of Suffolk. While other villagers were struggling to survive in the collapse of the wool trade, the Chaplins began to rebuild Old Hall. But both soon died and their son Benjamin gambled his estates away, dying almost penniless in Antigua.

Old Hall passed to the trusteeship of Henry Hankey, a London banker whose family had started as goldsmiths and pawnbrokers. Henry's son Joseph inherited the home and the business, invested heavily in the South Sea Company and, like Richard Rigby of Mistley, made a second fortune. Expansion began at Old Hall to accommodate Hankey's 13 children, of whom the eldest son Joseph Chaplin Hankey married a sugar heiress from Jamaica and added those estates to his Bergholt acres. Not surprisingly, his picture is owned by the National Portrait Gallery.

But in 1773 Hankey shot himself, aged 46, for reasons not recorded, and Old Hall's next known owner, in 1777, was Richard Rigby of Mistley, whose estates now covered 6,700 acres (2,700ha) and also included the manor of Commandree. The Godfrey family bought Old Hall in 1811, adding it to the three other Bergholt manors they already owned, and they sold it in 1849 on the death of Edward Godfrey's widow, the dowager Countess of Morton. The buyers were a Benedictine order of nuns, staunch Catholics who had survived the years of persecution by fleeing to Belgium.

St Mary's Abbey. Old Hall's days of glory were finished. The Benedictines extended the property yet again, building more rooms for their nuns and creating a school for girls, with the workforce being recruited from the Catholic community. By 1861 there were the Abbess, 19 nuns, 21 scholars and 8 servants, but in 1876 the

Mistley Towers, the remains of an Adam-designed church.

Benedictines shut the school and became an enclosed order.

As contact lessened with the outside world, the nuns built an impenetrable enclosure fence and continued improving on the convent's interior, becoming self-supporting for food with their own bakery and brewery, dairy and butchery.

Enclosed order. Enclosed orders were not particularly popular in the outside world, as nobody trusted a community that was so secretive, particularly as it was Catholic. Many of the nuns enjoyed their time in the convent, and Brenda Gamlin who wrote the story of Old Hall (available at the hall for £2.50) recalls a 1982 meeting with such a nun from the 1930s.

The Escaped Nun. Inevitably, there were sisters who couldn't accept the rigours of a closed order. One such was Margaret Moult who entered the convent after her family had fallen on hard times and who later talked about her experiences at St Mary's. In her testimony the convent's domestic arrangements belonged more to Dickens's time than to the beginning of the 20th century, with kitchen maids scooping fat off the boiling bone soup and later using it to make pastry, even if it had gone sour in the meantime.

The nuns, she said, took their clothes off only to wash themselves; they wore the same heavy habit in the sweltering summer and in midwinter, and slept in it the year through. The clothes were washed at intervals of months, and the blankets once every quarter century.

For seven years Margaret Moult endured the rigours of a hostile

37

life, resenting the seemingly senseless rules that governed the nuns lives from reveille at 5am almost until midnight. She queried why the windows of the unheated workroom had to be wide open, even in midwinter; she questioned the hours spent kneeling in penance on a cold floor; finally she questioned her own vocation.

Prisoner. But she could not leave. Excuse after excuse was put in her path until she had only one option. Bribing a gardener, she escaped from the convent on a rainy night and hurried up the road to Manningtree Station, hiding in the ditch as pony carts passed; hiding, even, from the Abbess going in search of her. She managed to reach the station, borrowed the fare to London from the stationmaster Mr Swain, and for the next few months became a national figure as the scandal of convent life became known to an astounded public.

Her book, *The Escaped Nun,* published by Cassell & Co in 1911, was a big success, but Brenda Gamlin adds that the Protestant Truth Society commissioned the publication and had its own list of anti-Catholic titles – and it awarded stationmaster Swain a medal for helping Miss Moult.

Army of occupation. The sisters left the convent in May 1940 under the threat of German invasion which was expected to strike at Clacton-on-Sea; the Army moved in and used Old Hall as a transit camp with up to 400 troops at a time billeted there, but several soldiers suspected that at least one nun had stayed behind, in spirit if not in the flesh. One man's hair reputedly turned white overnight after ghostly hands stroked his face.

Friars. The Army left in October 1945 to be replaced by friars of the Franciscan Order, whose numbers soon swelled to 67, mostly students preparing to go abroad as missionaries. By the 1960s the enclosed order was being eased and the friary welcomed students to use its 30,000-volume library, but the pace of change was moving so fast that the Fransiscans soon found themselves in a theological backwater. In 1973 the remaining few went to the University of Kent, leaving just one friar to be watchman until the building could be deconsecrated and sold.

Unit One Suffolk Housing Association. The new owners were 15 families and several single people who bought the building collectively, to be occupied as a community – *not* a commune. At first some of the villagers were horrified, thinking of hippies and drug parties, but they changed their minds when they learned that teachers, local government officers and an accountant were among the members.

Officially Old Hall is now the Unit One Suffolk Housing Association, with family groups and individuals holding shares in the whole rather than owning or leasing their separate apartments. People can sell their way out of the association at the same level of the housing market at which they came in, and the only way in is to buy a share. Tom

Keating wanted to join, but couldn't afford it.

There is a hint of that original feudal society in the way Old Hall is run, as everybody is expected to contribute unpaid labour on the land, in the house, or even at the accounts. The community is as near self-supporting as possible, raising its own cattle and poultry, growing its own vegetables and corn, on its 65 acres (26ha) and baking its own bread. Most of the 40 or so adult members are involved in ecological or conservation issues, growing their food organically, but the community is not like a kibbutz, nor does it have political or religious sympathies. It has no leader, being governed by genuine collective decision-making.

There are no set open days, but many visitors come by invitation to study a range of topics; some are interested in organic gardening but others want to see how the 'extended family' system, still common in Africa and Asia, can survive in modern, materialist Europe. If you want to know more, *write* to the Secretary, Old Hall Community, East Bergholt, Colchester, CO7 6TG.

Sexton Blake. If an artist is lucky and develops a distinctive style which catches the public's attention, he may make his reputation within 20 years. If he's unlucky, he may never achieve fame. Recognition came late for Constable, but Gainsborough and Munnings found it earlier in life.

It nearly eluded Tom Keating altogether. Keating had striven for years to get that essential acclaim, but in the fickle art world it continually eluded him. So, he reasoned, if the world didn't want Keatings, he would give it what it did want: Constables, Palmers, almost any artist you could name. Keating therefore became the artist *par excellence*, not only gifted with his own style, but able to imitate others' work. And still the world ignored him.

He came to East Bergholt, looking for success where Constable had found it. He exhibited Keating originals at the art gallery opposite the village post office, now Stour Crafts, but his main legitimate income was from restoring old masters while he made a small not-so-legitimate living by selling 'Sexton Blakes,' his word for 'fakes.'

Suddenly the news broke in the art world: Keating was a copier. People who had taken him their old masters suddenly wondered if they had received the originals back, or had Keating slipped them a Sexton Blake? Several customers knew they could never go to the police as the Inland Revenue would start asking awkward questions.

Fame at last. The scandal brought Keating the fame he desired, but it was fame as a copier of other painters' work rather than in his own right, although this called for far greater skill. He began selling Keating Palmers, Keating Constables, including a mirror image of the *Hay Wain*, and he had his own series on television.

Flatford Mill as seen from Willy Lott's Cottage.

But it was too late. He had wanted to buy his way into the Old Hall Community but couldn't raise the cash, so he rented a small house in Dedham. Christie's had a sale of some of his works in December 1983, then in September 1984 had a major sale of 205 Keatings in the manner of Dégas, van Gogh, Constable, Monet, Manet, Renoir, Palmer, Rembrandt and others. It was a huge success, with prices three times higher than expected, raising £274,000. But by then Keating was dead, aged 67.

In fairness to Keating I should explain that he never attempted to sell his Sexton Blakes as anything but copies, and an art expert could always recognise them from the originals. He was a brilliant copier, but he was not a forger.

Haunted pub. When I wrote the first edition of this book, the *Hare and Hounds* had been in the news for its ghost, called Fred, who allegedly ran across upstairs floors and through locked doors, who flushed the lavatory repeatedly, and who moved the bar furniture – and a customer – in full public view.

TOURIST INFORMATION

East Bergholt's **tourist office** opened for business at Easter 1990 in the Pot Hole, a pottery and craft shop opposite Old Hall; ✆0206.298161. It's now open Easter to late Sep, Sat-Thurs, 1030-1730, but the **shop is open** beyond these hours and dates. Pottery is made on the premises.

EAST BERGHOLT SHOPS. baker, butcher, pharmacy, DIY and hardware, Post Office stores, newsagent, coffee shop, Pot Hole crafts (see above), and Stour Crafts where Keating exhibited. **Pubs:** Beehive, Carriers' Arms, Hare and Hounds, King's Head, Red Lion.

FLATFORD

Flatford is the centre of Constable's Country and the focal point of the entire Stour valley, yet it is a tiny hamlet with just seven buildings: Flatford Mill, the original Constable family home; Willy Lott's Cottage, made famous by Constable's *Hay Wain;* Valley Farm, which also featured in Constable's work; the Granary Museum and house; Bridge Cottage, for **tourist information** and teas (Apr-May and Sep-Oct, Wed-Sun; Jun-Aug daily, 1000-1730); the Richardsons' bungalow behind the little kiosk; and the **public lavatories (and &)** on the car park for the disabled.

Access. Access is not easy. In your car, leave the main village street at Burnt Oak Corner near the King's Head pub and drive south for 750 yards (metres) along a narrow, one-way-traffic lane, and stop in the large parking area (£1 per car) for the final descent on foot (250yds to Bridge Cottage, 500yds to Willy Lott's Cottage). People with & badges may drive down to the lower car park; others risk a fine at busy times. Return from the main car park along 0.8 miles (1.4km) of lane which meets the village street beside Old Hall and the towerless church. Near the end of the lane a gateway on the left frames the view that Constable caught in *The Cornfield*, his first picture to go to the National Gallery.

Warning. Don't try driving down during afternoons at peak summer weekends or on bank holidays; the car park is full and vehicles are lining the lane. Leave your car near the Red Lion and walk.

Flatford Mill. The mill was in ruins in 1689 when Abram Constable, John's grandfather, bought and restored it, cashing in on the barge trade coming down the Stour. After the Constable era and when railways began replacing waterborne traffic, business declined and the mill was sold, with two cottages and a meadow, for 2,000 guineas (£2,100) in 1846. It ceased grinding flour in 1901 and the machinery was taken out in 1908 with the property again beginning to show dereliction. A local benefactor restored it and Willy Lott's Cottage, then gave them to the National Trust in 1927. Both are still in trust ownership but neither is **open to members or to the public** as they are on lease to the Field Studies Council (see below). Stand near the FSC office – you may need to get permission – and turn towards Willy Lott's Cottage for the view immortalised in the *Hay Wain;* the cottage is in much better condition than it was in 1821. Constable put his hay wain (wagon) in the centre of the stream, showing how shallow it was;

indeed, the name Flatford is probably a corruption of *fleet ford,* 'fleet' being an old word for 'shallow.'

Cross the stream by the bridge for a view of the mill's other façade, probably more impressive as it includes the mill race and a larger pond.

Willy Lott's Cottage. You can walk up to the front gate of Willy Lott's Cottage, which now serves as an overspill dormitory for the FSC's students at Flatford Mill. I've been inside both buildings and I can report that the mill's interior is impressive, with heavy beams in the refectory and several other rooms, but I found the cottage uninspiring. Willy Lott worked on the river and is believed to have spent only four nights away from home in his 86 years.

Valley Farm. North of the mill, Valley Farm is a picturesque half-timbered building set amid beautiful gardens, and the subject of yet another Constable painting. It's the residence of the FSC warden and is also **closed to the public.**

The Granary Museum. The next building back along the lane is a large, tarred-timber granary built in 1740 and owned by the Constable family from 1765 to 1840. In 1800 it became a macaroni factory with a chimney 60ft (20m) tall.

It was restored in 1975-'76, its owners having difficulty in getting planning permission to convert it into a museum, the Granary Museum (✆0206.298111). The present owners, Derek and Margery Tripp, who moved here in 1985, open 1030 to dusk daily in summer and Christmas Day, according to the weather in winter, for 30p. The museum holds the ancient cycle collection of John Malseed of Dedham, plus many other relics of rural life before the motor age.

Ready for some light diversion? The owner told me that Lord Howard's fifth son scaled the castle walls at the Siege of Boulogne in 1544. When Henry VIII asked him how, the son replied: "I tripp'd up ye walls." The king said: "Then Tripp shall be thy name."

Bridge Cottage. The thatched Bridge Cottage, also owned by the National Trust, doubles as the tourist office (see above for times). &: wheelchairs *not provided.*

Bridge Cottage stands, as you may guess, beside the hump-back pedestrian-only bridge (maintenance vehicles cross it); on the bridge's other side you can **hire a rowing-boat** for £5 deposit plus £2 per half-hour, £3 per hour; capacity two adults or four youngsters. If nobody is in attendance, ask at the Granary Museum. A similar bridge appears in several Constable paintings but the present span was designed by Munnings.

No swimming. A notice warns that as there is sewage effluent in the river, don't swim. Leave it to the ducks.

The Richardsons' bungalow. The elderly Misses Richardson used to run the Flatford Tea Gardens in their more active days; their bungalow, behind the kiosk (open 1015), is now private. Years ago they had an old Ipswich trolleybus as part of their home, but it has since gone back to Ipswich for restoration and display. .

Flatford Lock. Cross the bridge to find this most celebrated lock on the River Stour, a late 1930s concrete replacement of the timber original that Constable knew. The River Stour Trust restored it and reopened it to small-boat navigation in 1975.

THE FIELD STUDIES COUNCIL

The Field Studies Council is a charity striving to promote 'environmental understanding to all' from its head office at Preston Montford, Montford Bridge, Shrewsbury, SY4 1HW (✆0743.850674). It has field centres at Malham Tarn, North Yorkshire; Drapers, Betws-y-Coed; Dale Fort near Haverfordwest, Dyfed; Orielton, 54 acres near Pembroke; Nettlecombe Court, Williton, near Taunton; Slapton Ley near Kingsbridge, Devon; Juniper Hall, in National Trust property near Box Hill, Dorking, Surrey; the Epping Forest day centre near Loughton; Preston Montford; and Flatford Mill here in Suffolk.

Flatford Mill Field Centre. The Flatford Mill Field Centre, East Bergholt, Colchester, CO7 6UL (the mail is delivered from Essex), ✆0206.298283, follows the FSC pattern by offering week-long and weekend courses usually aimed at people older than 16, individually, in families, or in groups – but half of Flatford's visitors are students.

The Granary Museum at Flatford.

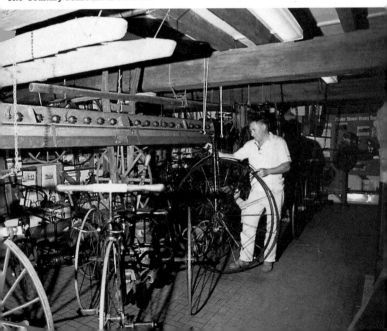

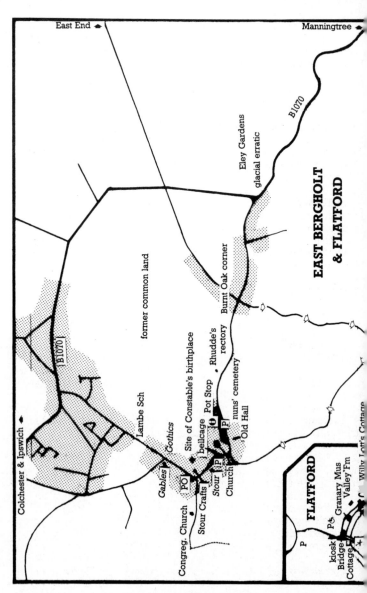

EAST BERGHOLT & FLATFORD

East End

Manningtree

B1070

Eley Gardens

glacial erratic

Colchester & Ipswich

B1070

former common land

Burnt Oak corner

Lambe Sch

Gables

Gothics

Site of Constable's birthplace

Pot Stop

Rhudde's rectory

PO

Congreg. Church

Stour Crafts

bellcage

Stour

Church

nuns' cemetery

Old Hall

FLATFORD

P

kiosk

Bridge

Cottage

Granary Mus

Valley Fm

Willy Lott's Cottage

The courses on offer cover birds and animals, photography and crafts, ecology and conservation, archaeology and architecture, flowers, and painting, with a season starting in mid February and running through to early December.

Within those courses, sample subjects at Flatford include: Constable Country from a bike; tracing the history of your home; painting in watercolours; the Suffolk Stour from source to sea; a weekend on spiders; five Suffolk villages; practical hedgelaying; and many others, with painting taking prominence.

Fees range from around £80 for weekend courses to £200 for a week-long course in oil-painting, and include food, transport on the course, accommodation – either in the mill or in Willy Lott's Cottage – but excludes materials and transport to the centre.

CATTAWADE

Cattawade marks the spot where the freshwater Stour meets the tidal estuary, the name probably coming from *cat's wade,* hinting at the depth of water at low tide. The barrage was built in 1971, with the River Stour Trust later adding the boat rollers that allow dinghies to graduate from fresh water to salt.

DEDHAM

Dedham is not only the most popular village in Constable's Country, it is also the most popular in the Stour valley, judged by the number of motorists looking for a parking space in summer.

Parking. Space, with no time limit, is provided in front of the church, on the square in front of the pharmacy, and by the old Grammar School, but at weekends and at any time in summer you need to be there early. Other parking is available north of the village centre, on the right of the B1029 by the Mallard Restaurant, and on the left by the former mill.

Wool town. Dedham is an old wool town. The Earl of Suffolk had a fulling mill (for cleaning the cloth, using a clay known as fuller's earth) in the village as far back as 1382, and over the centuries the market here – held on the wide main street and where part of the churchyard now is – grew in importance, but was never among the main centres of commerce and never had its own particular brand of material. Kersey in Suffolk, for example, produced a heavy broadloom cloth called kersey or carsey; worsted originated in the Norfolk village of Worstead; and abroad, cashmere came from the Kashmir, calico was the product of Calicut (Calcutta) and damask that of Damascus. And in more recent times, the French *serge de Nîmes* corrupted its name to denim.

Flemish Houses. There were several migrations of Flemish and Huguenot weavers into eastern England, usually as a result of

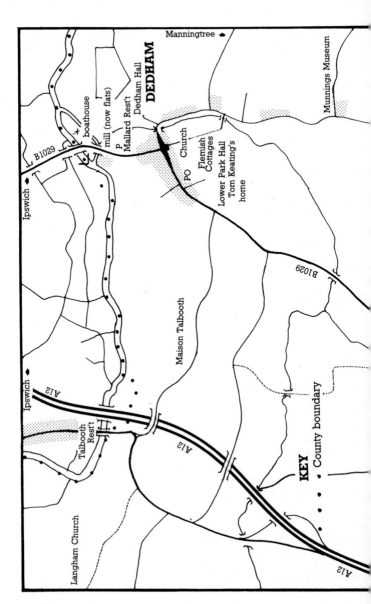

persecution at home; the so-called Flemish Houses a short walk south of the church across the playing fields, were in reality a 'bay and say' factory, producing material of specific type. Restored by the present owner, the houses are *not* open, but the gardens frequently are.

Princel Lane. Until recently, the last remnants of other weavers' cottages were visible at the bottom of Princel Lane, opposite the post office; this lane, now a dead end, led out across the water meadows to the river.

Marlborough Head. Go to the beautifully picturesque and rambling Marlborough Head inn opposite the church, and in the lounge at the front of the building look at the heavy beams across the ceiling. During the years of wool wealth, a massive hook in these beams was used for weighing fleeces and sacks of wool.

And outside in the marketplace, the Dedham Church Lectureship was founded in 1578, which meant the vicar had to ring the church bell and preach to the traders before business could begin. Now there is neither market nor lecture, and the bell is no longer rung at 0800 every Tuesday.

St Mary's Church. Dedham's Church of St Mary is smart and well-maintained, as befits a church that is occasionally featured on radio or television at festive occasions. Founded by cloth manufacturers Thomas Webbe and his son, whose trade marks join the Tudor rose on a carving on the tower, its main external feature is the carriageway which goes through the tower at ground level without entering the nave.

Erratic. Outside, by the south wall, stands an unusual gravestone, a glacial erratic which Edward Wood found with his plough in some unrecorded field. This relic of the Ice Ages now serves as the simple and undated headstone to Edward *and Martha His Wife.*

American connection. Building began in 1492, the year Columbus discovered America, and inside there are even stronger links with the New World. If you come from Devon you will doubtless claim that the Pilgrim Fathers sailed from Plymouth. The truth is that the 150-ton *Mayflower* was probably built in Harwich and had long traded on the east coast. She probably began her voyage at Rotherhithe, the home of her skipper Christopher Jones who was born in Harwich. She put into Southampton to pick up more passengers, and she called in at Plymouth only because her sailing companion the *Speedwell* had started to fall apart and could't make the Atlantic crossing.

The Dissenters, who became the Pilgrim Fathers, had been at their most vociferous in the eastern counties and the *Mayflower* had aboard more people from Dedham than from any other community in England. So why would they have travelled overland to Devon?

Pew carvings. It's no surprise to find a Dedham in Massachusetts – it was originally called Contentment – and to learn that the people of

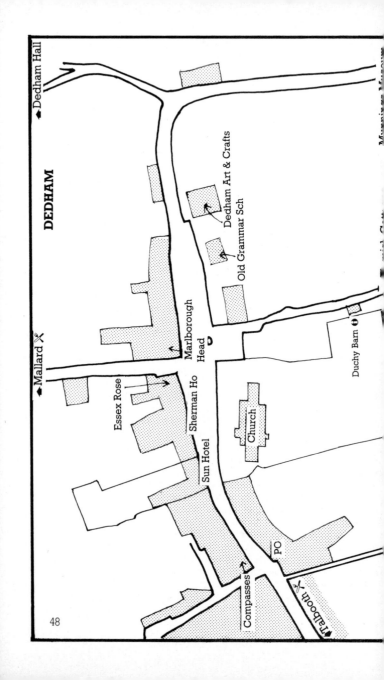

DEDHAM

← Dedham Hall

← Mallard ✕

Marlborough Head

Dedham Art & Crafts

Old Grammar Sch

Essex Rose

Sherman Ho

Sun Hotel

Church

Duchy Barn

PO

Compasses

✕ Talbooth →

Dedham's main street, with Sherman House and the Marlborough Head.

Kersey is renowned for its ford.

Hadleigh Church and Deanery Tower.

Long Melford's church seen across the village green.

The charm of East Anglia: this is a normal day in Nayland.

this Dedham gave more that £1,000 for the restoration of St Mary's Church in 1967. Now go to the last row of pews in the church and find the arms of the United States (1772 version) carved in the pew on the right. Study the delicate carvings in the back panels, from right to left: the torch of learning, an original settler house, the Great Seal of Massachusetts, the *Mayflower*, the first house of worship in Massachusetts, and finally a monogram of the two Ds and a cross.

Elsewhere, a wall tablet to the memory of *Judith Eyre...who died much lamented in the 35th Year of her Age in consequence of having accidentally swallow'd a Pin*, gives us a problem. The pin was in a Christmas pudding, which fits the date of Judith's death on *January 23rd 1747/8,* the uncertainty about the year probably anticipating the adoption of the Gregorian Calendar in England in 1752 when 10 days were lost from the older Julian reckoning. But there should have been no doubt about the *year*: it was the *day* that changed.

Sherman House. Opposite the church stands the elegant, early-18th cent Sherman House built on the site of a school founded in 1599 for teaching poor men's children to read and write. A later member of the Sherman family, Samuel, was aboard the *Mayflower* and settled in Contentment, Mass. One of his descendants became a hero in the American Civil War, and the Sherman tank of World War Two took its name from him.

Sherman's school wasn't the first in the village; by 1571 the Grammar School was already functioning, with a Sherman among its governors. Constable later attended this school with indifferent results, and today a selection of pupils' graffiti can still be seen carved in the bricks by the door, while a plaque over it says *Thomas Grimwood Hujus Scolae Magister 1732* – T Grimwood was the master of this school. The building is now the privately-owned Well House.

Miss Scarlin's school. In 1763 yet another school was planned. The *Ipswich Journal* carried this advertisement:

> Miss Scarlin intends to open her BOARDING-SCHOOL at Dedham on Tuesday the 14th Instant, when she hopes to receive those young Ladies whose Friends design to favour her with their Encouragement, who may depend upon her utmost Care & Endeavours to deserve it.

To labour too long on schools may give an unbalanced picture of Dedham and the life of the times. In that same year the *Ipswich Journal* carried another announcement:

> Whereas Thomas Howard, Son of Sarah Howard of Dedham, Essex, Apprentice to Philip Oriel, Stationer, in Aldersgate Street, London, ran away from his said Master's Service on Sunday April 24 last, and has since been heard of at Dedham aforesaid; This is to give Notice to all Persons whatsoever not to trust him with any Money &c on my Account, on any Pretence whatever. Whosoever harbours or employs him on any Account shall immediately be prosecuted with the utmost Severity of the Law. He is a strong, well-set Lad, about eighteen Years of Age, and wears his own Hair. He never had the Small-pox.

Workhouse. There was also a workhouse in the village, probably at the time when poor Thomas Howard was on the run. The brickwork had the inscription 1725 and the initials JG, which are believed to stand for James Godherd, the churchwarden of the time. His fellow warden was John Freeman who in 1730 gave lands and £145 in cash to build a house 'for lodging, maintaining and employing the poor of the Parish.' The workhouse survives, a picturesque building at the entrance to the road leading to the Flemish Cottages – but it's now called Weavershed House.

The Sun. Dedham has its share of ghost stories, particularly at The Sun, a former coaching house opposite the church. For as long as people can remember, there have been reports of sightings of the ghost of a young woman sitting on the stairs and crying, or walking in a first-floor room overlooking the road.

Writers of guide books normally don't get involved with what they report, but here's an exception. In the late 1970s I began some

Sherman House in Dedham has connections with a World War Two tank.

psychic research for a *Harwich and Manningtree Standard* feature, and I found myself haunted, day and night, for weeks, by the spirit of a young woman. "You must know, I am with you, always," she told me through a medium. Among the other information to come from that same source was that her name was Elsa, that she was the daughter of a Flemish weaver in Dedham, and that she had been burned to death in 1763, falsely accused of witchraft. "I was *not* a witch!"

Elsa's Room. I did a great deal of research on the subject of ghosts – I didn't believe in them at the time – and of witchcraft in general before concluding that Elsa's spirit was genuine, that in life she had been a serving maid at The Sun, and her death had probably occurred in the inn yard; the *Ipswich Journal* reported that a man in Suffolk was condemned to death by fire in that same year after being convicted of murder.

It was fairly obvious: my Elsa was the crying ghost on The Sun staircase, which is why the inn now has the name *Elsa's Room* on the door of that front bedroom, the best accommodation in the hotel and now furnished with a four-poster bed.

The Ghost Who Loved Me. I wrote the story of Elsa in a Corgi paperback, *The Ghost At My Shoulder,* and 10 years later I went back to find out why it was I whom Elsa had contacted. Having had thrust upon me the proof that ghosts exist, I found my own proof in the theory of reincarnation – that we may be born again into another body. If so, perhaps this present life is a reincarnation; have we been this way before?

Bit by bit I built up an incredible story, but equally true. According to Elsa and to other psychic sources, I had been a tax-gatherer back in 1763 and made calls at Dedham where I met her and fell in love. I agreed to take her away from the village, but as I already had a wife and family I didn't keep the promise. Elsa did – and the village women, jealous of her beauty and seeing her spurned, ganged up on her and burned her to death. Her ghost then waited tearfully for me in The Sun until finally we were reunited 225 years later. This story is also in print: *The Ghost Who Loved Me*, published by Heritage House in hardback.

And now for something completely different.

Dedham Art and Craft Centre. You'd like to buy some health food? Visit a toy museum? See potters and painters at work? Have some knitwear made to your design? Then call in at the Dedham Art and Craft Centre (✆0206.322666), admission 30p (senior citizens 20p), which Sandy Collier and Jeremy Parker created in 1984 in the shell of the old **United Reform Church**; its foundation stone was laid on 26 October 1871 by Minister Ebenezer Evans.

The Craft Centre is now a light and airy place on three floors, open daily 1000-1700 except Mondays Jan-Mar, where you can meet **resident artists** Terry Jeffrey, Brian Argent Smith and unrelated Kenneth Smith, visit Maureen and Geoff Theobald's **family restaurant** and health food shop (lunches 1200-1400, coaches by appointment; ✆0206.322677), and admire the exhibits in Joy Parkin's **toy museum,** (open 1030-1300, 1400-1700 daily except Mon and Fri). You can also have your barometer repaired, buy an antique map, some reproduction furniture, soft or wooden toys, handpainted glass, dried flowers, craft jewellery, and picture frames.

Tom Keating. Half a mile from the church along the B1029 to Ardleigh, Lower Park is a long-established country mansion. At the bottom of its driveway stands a small cottage usually occupied on short-term tenancies. Its most notable tenant was the painter whom the art world ignored at its peril, Tom Keating. Neither the cottage nor the main house is open to the public.

Munnings Museum. Go east out of the village along Brook Street, turning right by the entrance to Dedham Hall, and you soon reach Castle House, the home of Sir Alfred Munnings until his death in 1959, and now a museum of his life and work.

Alfred Munnings was born on 8 October 1878, the second son of a miller at Mendham, in the Waveney valley. He studied at Framlingham College before beginning an apprenticeship to a Norwich printer where he made a reputation as the designer of posters for Caley's Chocolates.

John Tomkins, one of Caley's directors, encouraged young Munnings and was his first patron, yet at the age of 19 during his apprenticeship Munnings had a picture accepted by the Royal Academy, the first of 230. Life for him was to be vastly different from that of Constable and Keating although an accident blinded his right eye when he was 20.

After his time with the printers, Munnings moved back to Mendham and his first studio where he began painting horses, local characters and landscapes. He moved on to the artists' mecca at Newlyn, added to his reputation by painting the Hampshire hop-pickers, and in 1918 became an official war artist with the Canadian Cavalry.

Castle House. The following year he bought Castle House, Dedham, "the house of my dreams," to which he took his bride, Mrs Violet McBride, in 1920; a widow, she had ridden the winner of the Cheltenham Gold Cup. With horses now firmly established in his life, Munnings spent the next 20 years travelling on commissions, with racing a major theme – but he was always ready to come home to Dedham.

1944 was an excellent year for him; he was knighted, and elected president of the Royal Academy, but his five year presidency was marked by some controversy on his opinion that much modern art was a confidence trick on the public. His wife had commented after the wedding that Alfred would henceforth have to paint for money and, despite sticking to traditional subjects, his works commanded the highest prices for a living British artist.

After his death, Lady Munnings carried out his wishes by turning Castle House into a museum, opening in 1965 with all Munnings's unsold paintings on display. Two galleries have been added to the **museum,** which also holds the family furniture. It's open May-early Oct, Sun, Wed, bank holiday Mon, (plus Thurs and Sat in Aug), 1400-1700, for £2, children 25p. ✆0206.322127.

The Dedham Vale Society. Alfred Munnings was the Dedham Vale Society's founder president in 1938, with Raymond Erith as chairman. Having saved the Sun Inn (chapter 1), the society was consulted in 1939 on the route of the Stratford bypass, then in 1946 had to fight the water authority's proposed 12-acre (4.8ha) reservoir near Dedham. In 1963 the society stopped a line of 132Kv pylons in the lower valley, and fought plans for overspill populations in 1964. Local architect Raymond Erith, RA, is best known for his restoration work at 10, 11 and 12 Downing St, London.

Dedham Hall. At the bend in Brook Street, near the craft centre, a lane leads up to Dedham Hall, a house standing in five acres (2ha) which is now a small hotel, the Fountain House Restaurant recommended by Egon Ronay and others, and a residential school for painters. You can book in for week-long courses from early March to late October for tuition in oils or watercolour; write to Dedham Hall, Brook St, Dedham, Colchester, CO7 6AD, or ✆0206.323027.

Dedham Mill. Dedham Mill was a corn and fulling mill, the foundation of the village's wealth until the late 18th cent. It closed in the 1980s and has now been converted to luxury apartments; the National Rivers Authority completed a rising gate to control the river level at nearby **Dedham Lock** in 1990. You can **hire boats** here for £2.50 half-hour, £4 hour, plus £10 deposit.

Talbooth. Between Dedham and Stratford St Mary are two of the smartest hotels in the area, **Maison Talbooth** and the **Dedham Vale Hotel,** both owned and run by the Milsom family. Maison Talbooth was a Victorian country house and enjoys excellent views across Dedham Vale, while the virginia-creeper-covered Dedham Vale Hotel recaptures an Edwardian atmosphere in its elegant Terrace Restaurant.

The Milsom family also owns **Le Talbooth,** a riverside restaurant in Stratford St Mary with an Egon Ronay two-star rating. The original building is in the middle distance of Constable's *Vale of Dedham* where it had served as a toll booth since 1695; later it was the home of a Flemish weaver – the Weaver's Room is one of the attractions of today's restaurant – and an auction notice of 1928 called it Limekiln Cottage. By 1935 it was derelict, to be restored and extended by Gerald Milsom.

If you go to old Harwich, call in at the **Pier at Harwich,** a Milsom hotel with two restaurants and a view across the Stour to Shotley.

Dedham Rare Breed Centre. Do you fancy wandering around a working farm that is a haven for rare breeds of sheep, goats, cattle and pigs? Want to renew acquaintance with Gloucester old spots, Tamworths, Irish moils, dexters, longhorns, and the four-horned loghtan sheep from the Isle of Man? Then come to the 14-acre (5ha) Dedham Rare Breed Centre, access from near the car park on the lane to the river; open every day 1000-1730 for £3 (£1.80 children); ✆0206.322176 and ask for Peter Harris.

INFORMATION. The **Dedham Countryside Centre,** (✆0206.323447) down a path south of the war memorial, is a useful source of information about the area; open Easter-mid October Tues-Sat 1000-1300, 1400-1700 (open on Mon from 1 May), and May-Sep Sun 1400-1700. You'll also find books, postcards, maps, and displays by conservation-minded bodies such as the Suffolk Wildlife Trust, the Essex Naturalists' Trust, the River Stour Trust, the National Trust, and the Council for the Protection of Rural Essex.

SHOPS IN DEDHAM. Boutiques, bookshop, Co-op store, teashop and crafts, butcher, chinaware, florist, pharmacy, Post Office, hairdresser, antiques. **Pubs:** Marlborough Head, Rose and Crown, Sun.

STRATFORD St MARY

Historically, Stratford St Mary has always been a place to go *through* rather than *to*, as this was where the old Roman road – in Low Latin, the *strata* – forded the river at the Roman community of **Ad Ansam,** with the Medieval tollbooth (now Le Talbooth Restaurant) conveniently nearby. And when Thomas and Margaret Mors, who had made their money from the wool trade, built the Church of St Mary between 1499 and 1530 on the site of a much earlier church, they also had the traveller in mind.

Lettered church. There are several churches with with letters built into their stonework, but Stratford Church is the only one to have the complete alphabet, the pale limestone characters offset by the dark flint, like chalk on a blackboard. Why? Probably as a reminder to travellers to say their prayers daily; or maybe a reminder that as all the world's prayers are made up of these letters, to repeat the alphabet was as good as saying a prayer. And the old-time travellers might be in Colchester before they remembered what follows Y.

Look carefully and you may be able to read in the stones *Pray for the soulls of Edward Mors and Alys hys wyfe and all Chrysten sowlys, Anno Domini 1530.* They were probably Thomas Mors's parents.

Travellers. Some of those travellers were gosherds from Norwich and Ipswich taking their geese and turkeys to the London markets for Christmas; from August onwards the flocks, sometimes thousands strong, would be passing through Stratford on foot. To make the

M is for Mary, but other letters are difficult to decipher at Stratford St Mary.

journey more tolerable, the birds were induced to walk through warm pitch and then through sand, so their feet were tarred even if the roads were not.

Stratford today is even more easy to go through, since the opening of the bypass in 1966. Before that the village was a dreaded accident black spot, with many articulated lorries coming to grief on Gun Hill.

The ancient ford went centuries ago, but the river has been crossed by several bridges; an iron structure, opened in March 1876, was closed when it developed nasty cracks, and it was taken out of service in 1926. Exactly 100 years before that, Constable painted his *Dedham Vale*, which clearly shows a wooden span with timber supports rising from the river bed.

Stratford Mill. Constable did modern historians a favour by painting *Stratford Mill on the Stour,* and thus showing that the building had a large waterwheel. Five years later the mill was replaced by a six-storey building, but 21 years after that, with the repeal of the Corn Laws, the millers' heyday was over. The giant mill was demolished just after World War Two.

Pumping station. The present concrete pumping station in the village has the capacity to take 189,000 cubic metres of water daily from the Stour, and pump it south to Ardleigh Reservoir, from where it serves Colchester and district.

Priest's House. In Constable's day, two of the most intriguing houses in the village had plaster exteriors. The Priest's House and the Ancient House have had links with the Church for, during restoration in 1945 when the plaster fronts were removed, a series of carved panels came to light set in 14th-cent timberwork, which might mean these buildings are the oldest part of any non-secular structure in the Dedham Vale. But we must be careful, as most of the houses are obviously Tudor and the oldest house in England is in Little Wenham; see chapter 4.

Gallows Field. And a grim note. The land opposite the church is called Gallows Field. How many men and women condemned to die here would look at those letters on the church wall and remember to say their prayers?

SHOPS IN STRATFORD St MARY. General store, Post Office stores. **Pubs:** Anchor, Black Horse, King's Arms, Swan. **Restaurant:** Le Talbooth.

AND ELSEWHERE

Ardleigh. Midway between Dedham and Colchester lies Ardleigh, known locally as the home of television clean-up campaigner Mary Whitehouse, and for its reservoir, where you can go windsurfing. The

Essex Crown Vineyard in Crown Lane (CO7 7RB; ☎0206.230142) has six acres (2.4ha) of vines on the shore of Ardleigh Reservoir, with trout fishing and bird watching as extra attractions. Its open daily, Easter-Oct 1430-1800, free, but phone before you go.

Bentley. North-east of East Bergholt and on the edge of our map is the small village of Bentley which gained brief notoriety in the 1970s for the Suitcases Murder, when a dismembered body was found in two cases left at the roadside.

Signatures of Henry VIII and Elizabeth I, his daughter by Anne Boleyn, both written at the height of their power.

4: RUSTIC RIVER

Higham to Nayland, with Hadleigh

IN THIS LOWER-MIDDLE SECTION of its course, the River Stour flows through a beautiful valley whose sides are steep by East Anglian standards. The Essex side has two tiny villages and a scattering of hamlets, with orchards predominating; the Suffolk side has villages that are only slightly larger but which have interesting and gruesome stories to tell, while to the north, along the River Brett tributary, lies the historic market town of Hadleigh.

ESSEX: Langham and Boxted.

St Mary the Virgin's church in **Langham** and the farmhouse nearby, which was never the rectory, contrary to local belief, were the secret meeting-places of John Constable and his bride to be, Maria Bicknell, as Maria's grandfather-guardian, the rector of East Bergholt, disapproved of the courtship. In 1830 Constable painted *The Glebe Farm*, but in the following decade a large rectory was built to the south; this is now Glebe House, in private ownership since 1975.

Poor box? The church, with origins in the 12th cent, holds one of the oldest poor boxes in England, cut from a single piece of oak and measuring 4ft 7in (1m40) by 1ft 6in (45cm), with only a tiny cavity inside to take money. One version of the box's origins is that it dated from the Tudor poor laws, probably from the 1552 Act of Edward VI under which parishioners were *gently exhorted and admonished* to contribute to the needs of the poor, but the church's own suggestion is that the chest was made following Henry II's decree of 1166 to finance another crusade; for the record, in 1188 Henry imposed the 'Saladin tithe' of 10% of all property values – *tithe* means 'tenth' – and the Third Crusade left in 1189 (see Old Hall, East Bergholt). Whichever story is true, it does not hide the fact that the box was plundered at some unknown time.

A later example of charity is the small **Hurlock Schoolroom** in the churchyard, 'designed for the daily instruction of poor girls of this parish' and financed by Dr Hurlock, rector from 1831 to '47. It was the village Sunday School until the 1950s.

The Flemish Cottages at Dedham were really a 'bay and say' factory.

Lawa's People. Langham is recorded in Domesday as *Laingham*, which is claimed to mean 'the home of Lawa's people,' a distinction it shares with Lawford if both are correct. Walter Tirel held the manor for his father-in-law, Richard Fitzgilbert de Clare, who built Clare Castle. Tirel's son, Hugh de Poix, sold the manor in 1147 before going on the Second Crusade, and the lordship then progressed through the Neville family to the de la Poles, who provided the Earls of Suffolk. And when Edmund de la Pole was executed in 1513 the manor went to Henry VIII whose wives Catherine of Aragon and Jane Seymour held the patronage and appointed the rectors.

Boxted. Boxted's Norman church tower is believed to have more puddingstone in its construction than has any other tower in East Anglia. The Puritans added the dormer windows in the nave roof to break what they saw as an austere line, yet elsewhere they smashed beauty to leave austerity.

The Horkesleys. Great and Little Horkesley are tiny villages in the shadow of Colchester, but the former is built on a Roman road known today as The Causeway, and the latter had an important priory in the time of Henry I. Robert, son of Godebold, and his wife Beatrice, established the Priory of St Peter for monks of the Cluniac sect, owing allegiance to the great priory of Thetford. Wolsey suppressed it in 1525, to remove competition when he was trying to establish his college in Ipswich.

The Horkesley family held the manor from around 1200 to 1322, with some of their knights represented in the church by wooden effigies, their crossed legs showing that they went on crusade to the Holy Land.

Tiny **Wormingford** has The Crown and The Queen's Head pubs close together, the latter cleverly shown as a penny black stamp.

SUFFOLK: Higham and Thorington St.

Higham may almost be described as the village with nothing. It has no shop, no pub, no vicar for its church – but it has a post office.

Brigadier and Mrs Gurney of **Higham Lodge** have a private horse-race course in their grounds and play host to four point-to-point meetings a year at three-weekly intervals starting in mid-February; visiting teams usually come from the North Norfolk, the Waveney Valley, the Essex and Suffolk and the Eastern harriers. The Gurneys have self-catering cottages for rent (see chapter 9), and can arrange fishing on the Stour for guests – most of the river is controlled by angling clubs.

Higham's **Church of St Mary** is rather featureless; there are no brasses, it's small even for the 13th cent, and it is mostly built of flint with no embellishments. The main features are the grapevines and rosettes carved in the capitals in the nave, and the medieval carvings on the bench-ends.

Along the road north to Shelley and Layham you'll find **Teacaddy Cottage,** a house with curved end walls, just like a tea caddy.

Thorington Street. Two miles west of Higham, Thorington Street has a small reservoir down by the riverside, and another glacial erratic in the verge outside Thorington Hall; this particular one is believed to have been a boundary marker in Saxon times. The roadside Hall is a fine example of a 16th-cent gabled farmhouse, its most conspicuous feature being the six chimneys fused into one enormous stack 50ft (15m) high. In 1937, builders carrying out repairs in the main room found a 16th-cent shoe behind some ornamental plaster. The National Trust owns the property which is in the bed-and-breakfast business.

STOKE-by-NAYLAND

The main question to ask of Stoke-by-Nayland is: where is the monastery (in Old English, *stoc,*) from which the village took its name? The certainty is that there is not the slightest trace of a monastery today in this picturesque little village built on a Suffolk hillcrest.

L.S. Hartley, a local amateur archaeologist, claimed that there never was a *stoc*, merely the promise of one, and the story goes like this:

Danish invaders. The Saxon sisters Aethelflaed and Agelflaed received in their father's bequest a piece of land on which to build a monastery, and the money to pay for it. But one of the sisters married **Bryhthoth** (his name is spelled several ways), the Saxon earl or ealdorman who was killed at the Battle of Maldon in August 991 fighting the Danish invaders, and is buried at Ely Cathedral. As a result, Hartley claimed, the money for Stoke monastery was temporarily diverted to more pressing uses, the events of 1066 making the diversion a finality.

Royal connections. Stoke's greatest claim to fame is its association with Sir William de Tendryng, whose brass is in the village church although his body is buried at Holbrook, Suffolk. Sir William, whose family took its name from the Tendring Hundreds in north-east Essex, built Tendring Hall in Stoke, and was great-grandfather to Sir John Howard who later became the Duke of Norfolk and married Katharine Molyns in 1442.

This couple were grandparents of Anne Boleyn and Catherine Howard, two of the queens of Henry VIII; they were therefore great-grandparents to Anne's daughter, Queen Elizabeth I. Anne Boleyn has strong connections with Erwarton in Suffolk (see *Discover the Suffolk Coast*) as her heart was entombed in the local church, and she was born at Blickling Hall in Norfolk (see *Discover North Norfolk*).

Mannock. Away from the regal line, a brass in Latin verse in the church is epitaph to William Mannock who died in 1616 20 years after forfeiting two thirds of his estate for abandoning his faith; a touching contradiction in the north chapel is the elegant marble statue of a recumbent Sir Francis Mannock – was it his father? – of Danish descent, lord of the Manor of Gifford Hall who died in 1634 aged 49 and 'whose religious conversion made him reverenced of all.' Nearby **Gifford Hall** is not open to the public, and shouldn't be confused with Gifford's Hall north of Long Melford, a farm which is open to the public.

St Mary's Church. The 15th-cent St Mary's Church is of flint and mortar, typical of many financed by the wool trade, but the south porch has windows from previous centuries hinting that it once formed part of an earlier church on this site – and the site of St Mary's is outstanding, its 120ft (36m) tower commanding the views of the Stour to the south and of Polstead to the north, with some of the most rugged and impressive half-timbered medieval cottages of the eastern counties by its western wall. Inside, the 19th-cent pulpit is carved from Caen and Languedoc stone which some people think was surplus material from Mistley's new church.

Camping Field. Stoke's Camping Field, recently cultivated for the first time in history, was the village recreation ground for centuries and had no connection with camping. Its name came from the Old English or Saxon game of *kampen,* in which the contestants fought each other in a kind of fanatic Rugby, probably without the excuse of chasing a ball. The name has links with modern German *Kampfenfeld,* 'fighting field.'

Scotland Street. And there's another of those glacial erratics at Scotland Hall, a farm on Scotland Street, the oddly-named road wandering east to **Withermarsh Green.** Around 8ft by 3ft (2.4m by 1m), it has remained where the retreating glaciers left it.

STOKE-by-NAYLAND SHOPS. There are two general stores near the pubs. **Pubs:** Angel, Black Horse, Crown.

LEAVENHEATH

Leavenheath is one of those villages that has almost vanished, but within the parish boundary are a smart golf course and a commercial enterprise that was featured on BBC television in 1990. And their stories are connected.

Stoke-by-Nayland Golf Club. The golf club, on the B1068 west of Stoke-by-Nayland, opened with the Gainsborough course in 1972 and added the Constable course in 1979; both are 18-hole with a par of 72 and, although there's a waiting-list for membership, visitors can pay a greens fee for a day's game, with equipment available on hire. The club's owner is Boxford and Suffolk Farms which, back in the 1950s, decided to squeeze the juice from its unsaleable apples.

Copella. The fruit-juice business grew steadily until it became an enterprise in its own right, named Copella from the Cox's Orange Pippin apples that formed the majority of its output. From a simple

These charming old houses are at Stoke-by-Nayland.

hand press the business has moved on to total automation, squeezing 8,800,000 gallons (40,000,000 litres) in 1989 and controlling six percent of the British pure juice market.

In 1969 Copella began optionally adding blackcurrant, pear, guava and strawberry to its apple juice, but it has stayed true to its original policy of not adding preservatives, sugar, colour, or water; the juice is preserved only by pasteurisation. Business grew, and Copella non-alcoholic juice is now distributed through many supermarket chains as well as Harrods, Holland and Barrett, Forte hotels and the National Trust.

But in the late 1980s the company ran into administrative problems as it was no longer compatible with its Suffolk farm beginnings. The television programme *Troubleshooters* gave the directors several options, and they chose to sell half the company to Taunton Cider to get better and cheaper distribution. In April 1991 Taunton Cider bought the remaining half of Copella's shares.

The **farm shop** sells Copella products Mon-Fri 0900-1600; for more information write Hill Farm, Boxford, CO6 5NY or ✆0787.210348.

BOXFORD

The A1071 now bypasses beautiful Boxford, allowing it to resume normal life astride the River Box, a tiny tributary of the Stour. Boxford, not connected with Boxted in Essex, lost its ford many years ago with the growth of traffic on the Sudbury-to-Hadleigh road.

A tablet in St Mary's Church remembers *Elizabeth Hyam of this Parish, for the fourth time Widow; who by a Fall, that brought on a Mortification, was at last hastened to her End, on the 4th May 1748 in her 113th year.*

Boxford shops; three general stores. **Pubs:** Compasses, Fleece, White Hart, Swan.

Groton. A mile north, Groton village is a collection of tiny hamlets centred on the church, the Fox and Hounds pub, and Groton Hall, former home of John Winthrop, lord of the manor who gave up his career as Justice of the Peace, sailed with the Pilgrim Fathers aboard the *Mayflower*, and became the first governor of Massachusetts.

POLSTEAD

Mention Polstead to the older generation and most people automatically remember the **Murder in the Red Barn,** a 19th-cent scandal that still brings hundreds of visitors each year to this tiny village.

Maria Marten. Maria Marten was the oldest daughter of the village molecatcher, and well eductated for the early 19th cent. But she was of far easier virtue than the average girl of her day, having borne three if not four illegitimate children to three fathers.

In 1827 Maria went missing, and was soon presumed to have been murdered, but almost a year passed before there was any clue. And then Maria's stepmother saw the grave in a dream in such detail that she could recognise the location: in the earth floor of the red barn to the east of the village.

When the body was found, just as she had described, and murder was established, the obvious suspect was William Corder, father of Maria's last child and uncle to her first.

The case aroused immense public interest, particularly in the manner in which Maria's body had been located – modern dream interpretation dates from this incident – and Corder was condemned in the public eye even before the case came to the assizes at Bury St Edmunds.

William Corder. Several thousand people visited Polstead and trekked on to Bury for the trial; peep shows and mummer's plays, throughout England and even outside the courtroom, all told of Corder's guilt in murdering his mistress.

Yet the trial never touched on the vital issues of how Maria died – by stabbing, strangulation, shooting or suffocation – although Corder's knife and a brace of his pistols are in the Moyses Hall Museum in Bury. Indeed, the trial never even settled the issue of whether Corder merely wounded Maria, with another person finishing her off.

Corder, of course, was found guilty, and hanged, but the grisliest part of the story belongs with Corder rather than with his alleged

Dedham's Church of St Mary in early spring.

This gaunt treadmill crane at Harwich is the only one in Britain.

The John Constable window in East Bergholt church.

THE GRACE OF GOD WAS UPON HIM   HE TOOK HER UNTO HIS OWN HOME

DRY OF JOHN CONSTABLE R.A   BORN IN THIS PARISH 1776 DIED 18

Lavenham's Guildhall is a monument to its medieval builders.

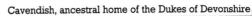

Cavendish, ancestral home of the Dukes of Devonshire

victim. His body was sent to the West Suffolk General Hospital in Bury St Edmunds where it was dissected, according to the custom of the day, and *then* put on public display in a glass case with a collection box underneath. The hospital used the skeleton for many years in anatomy lessons before passing it to the Royal College of Surgeons in October 1949 where it stands in the private museum.

Bookbinding. A reporter from *The Times* who covered the trial put his slanted version in a book, one copy of which was bound in a segment of pickled skin taken from Corder's body; this volume is still kept in the Moyses Hall Museum, with a death mask.

Legend claims that Corder was beheaded and his skull had the only decent burial of any part of his anatomy, being smuggled in with a corpse in an undeclared grave – but this last step was taken only after a series of poltergeist manifestations and other ill luck had troubled the people who had given the skull a home. However, the College of Surgeons says Corder seems to be wearing his own skull.

The red barn burned down in 1842, but Maria's birthplace can still be seen in Marten's Lane, and Corder's house is still in the main street. The full story is in *The Red Barn Mystery*, by McCormick, published by John Long in 1967.

Polstead has other claims to fame. Its pond, which threatens to flood the road, probably explains the village name as *pondsted*, and the village was long known for its cherry fair. There's an enormous and very dead **gospel oak** in the village, with a young tree growing from the remains, and the village church has a rare **Breeches Bible,** a version of the Holy Book which claims that Adam wore breeches rather than that he merely covered his nakedness. And if you're looking for another connection with murder, this village is home to Ruth Rendell the writer of whodunits.

Pub: The Cock, at the top end of the village.

NAYLAND

John Constable's aunt, who lived in Nayland, asked him to paint a picture for the parish church as he had already done one for Brantham. The result, *Christ Blessing the Elements* – the bread and wine – is far from being among his best, but it has formed the altar piece since 1809 and is still in place, despite having been stolen several times; nowadays it's guarded by the latest electronic devices.

Nayland Church. The village church of St James is unusual in the eastern counties for having a spire instead of a tower, and an unusual story to explain it. The stumpy tower that stands underneath was badly shaken in the Great Essex Earthquake which struck at 0920 on 22 April 1884 and in the 1960s was declared too dangerous for the bells to be rung. So the church authorities reduced the height of the tower, built the steeple, and rehung the bells in 1974.

Pargeting – ornate plasterwork – in the centre of old Hadleigh.

The spire looks awkward – even the authorities admit it – but inside, the building is an average example of a 15th-cent Perpendicular church which, in this instance, was paid for by the parishioners to replace a 13th-cent chapel. At least seven brasses were laid in the floor of the nave, marking the tombs of important clothmakers in the town, but when the trade moved to Yorkshire and depression hit Suffolk, the brasses vanished. Today there's not even a record of whom they commemorated.

Bats. While you're in the church, look for the owl perched near the top of a window in the nave. The bird is stuffed and has been on duty since the 1960s, as no other device would persusade a colony of bats to leave.

Wool. Nayland could surely afford the expense of a new church, as records from 1552 show there were 14 clothmakers, nine shearmen, eight weavers and four fullers here. Nayland's cloth was frequently dyed in woad, giving it a blueish colour which was fixed by immersion in a solution of alum (aluminium or potassium sulphate). The cloth trade was still struggling to survive in 1970, with a sheet and shirt manufacturer in business at the top of Fen Street.

Fen Street The River Stour splits into two immediately before reaching Nayland, with the northern course, now the county boundary, running under the former shirt factory, going over a 4ft (1.2m) weir hidden beneath the building, then gliding smoothly along Fen Street, where the houses on the Suffolk side have individual footbridges linking them with the road on the Essex bank; come here in spring or summer for a true floral delight.

The existence of that other branch of the Stour means that Nayland is on an island: indeed, the Old English name for the community was *atten Eiland*, 'to the island,' the N having changed allegiance over the centuries. *Atte* is a rare prefix, but it is still seen in the London borough of Havering-atte-Bower, and in the family name *atte lea*, 'to the meadow,' corrupted to Attlee as in the post-war prime minister.

William Abell. There's more fun with words when you consider how William Abell is best remembered. Abell built a timber bridge over the river in the early 16th cent, providing funds for its maintenance 'in perpetuity.' The bridge survived until 1771 when its brick replacement had the letter A and the shape of a bell carved in the keystone. This bridge was outdated in the 1950s because it was too narrow, but the 'A bell' carving was included on the east side of the third structure, today's bridge. By the way – the contractors found enough World War Two explosive buried in the 1771 structure to destroy it at the touch of a button.

Abell built the village hall in 1510, putting it across the main road and so forcing the horse-and-cart traffic of the day to zigzag through the backstreets – which explains why the village's main street still has an irregular building line. This road carried increasingly heavy traffic until the bypass – and a new bridge – came in 1969-'70.

Queen Anne. And while you're in the main street, glance at the Georgian obelisk which tells you London is 55 miles away, then take a closer look at the leaning Queen Anne doorway on a house in Alston Court, near Church Mews.

Press Gang. The Anchor pub, down by Bell Bridge, has a mention in English history as the last known place where the Press Gang operated. Edward III started the Commission of Impressment in 1355 to find infantrymen and sailors; Parliament declared the press gang illegal in 1641, yet it survived until the Napoleonic Wars, conscripting men off the streets to five years' service aboard ship without the option – without even having a chance to say farewell to their families.

Court Knoll. The first known human settlement at Nayland lies where the two branches of the Stour reunite. This is Court Knoll, a site that was occupied for several thousand years; a Bronze Age urn from here is in Colchester's Castle Museum, and there is evidence of a kitchen midden in use shortly after the Norman Conquest. Don't try visiting the knoll; it's on private farmland and the most anybody can see is faint crop markings from the air.

SHOPS IN NAYLAND.

Bookshop, wholefoods, butcher, hairdresser, general stores, Post Office stores. **Pubs:** Anchor, White Hart.

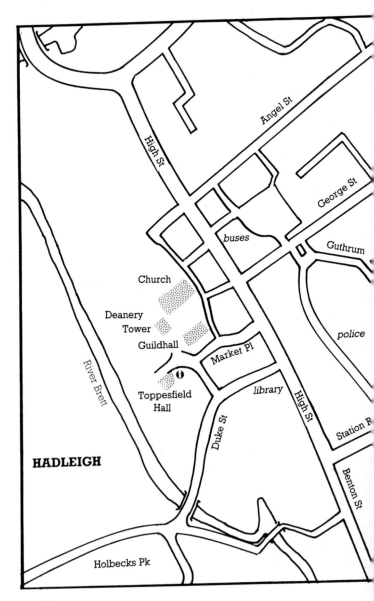

HADLEIGH

Hadleigh, a picturesque market town on the River Brett, a tributary of the Stour, was a thriving Saxon town in the 5th cent, its name probably suggesting the heathland of the area. The Saxons had come from *Sachsen,* Saxony, but those in the eastern part of this island were driven out by a later insurge of the Angles, who came from *Angeln,* a tiny district north of Hamburg; together they were to form the Anglo-Saxons, later to become the English – but not yet.

The Danish pirate Goturm conquered the territory of the still-pagan East Angles in 870 and had become their king, but he was having problems with his West Saxon neighbours led by the redoutable Alfred, King of Wessex. Fifteen years later Goturm's ships met Alfred's tiny fleet in what was to be the first recorded naval battle in British waters which also gave us the first mention of Harwich Harbour – that was where the fleets met – and which gave Shotley Spit (the peninsula opposite Harwich) the name of Bloody Point.

Goturm lost the battle, accepted baptism into Christianity, and went back to Hadleigh to build a tiny church; if any of it remains, it lies deep in the modern churchyard with the bones of Goturm himself, who died in 890. English history knows the King of the Angles as **Guthrum,** but Shetland history remembers him by his Danish name, and Goturm's Hole, a cave in a bleak Shetland cliff, marks the spot where he first landed in Britain.

Beortnoth. In 991 the Danes attacked East Anglia once again, sailing up the Blackwater where they had a major battle near Maldon, cruising up the Stour and burning the community now called Brantham, and causing severe damage elsewhere. Beortnoth, the Ealdorman (leader, chief, and origin of the title 'alderman') of East Anglia, was among the victims of the Maldon massacre, leaving his estates at Hadleigh to pass to the **Archbishop of Canterbury;** as a result the town had the title of 'Archbishop's Peculiar' until 1858. You may find Beortnoth mentioned in several accounts of East Anglian history, but you'll probably never see a consistent spelling of his name.

Danish interlude. After Maldon, the Danes seized much of eastern England, and exacted the *Danegeld* or land tax in 1001, worth around £300,000 in today's money. Ethelred the Unready ordered the massacre of the Danes in November 1002 which led to Sven Forkbeard plundering the country in revenge. Ethelred fled to Normandy until Sven died, but the Danes proclaimed Knut (Canute) as king of Anglia while Edmund Ironside was king of the remainder of England. Knut defeated Edmund in 1016 and at the age of 22 ruled all the country until his premature death in 1035, when Harthaknut (Hardicanute) took the south and east and Harald Harefoot the north.

Edward the Confessor reunited the kingdom in 1042 but his successor, Harold Godwineson, was forced to defeat a Norwegian attack in the north only to die, weeks later, at the Norman invasion in the south, on 14 October, 1066.

Hadleigh Church. Guthrum's Anglo-Saxon church lasted into the 12th cent, to be rebuilt and enlarged three times in the next three centuries as sheep grazing began to replace crop growing, and wool became the generator of the nation's wealth. The present church is 15th-cent, built from limestone and unbroken knobs of flint, and with a spire 71ft (21.6m) from base to tip, the tip being 135ft (41m) above ground. Look carefully and you will see a gentle twist, showing that the original timbers were not straight. And Guthrum? His 14th-cent tomb is in the 15th-cent church, but nobody knows where his bones really lie.

The 15th cent was the time of Hadleigh's greatest wealth, and most of the town's story of that time is recorded in the impressive cluster of buildings between the present High Street and the river.

Guildhall. Possibly the most imposing structure is the Guildhall, just across the churchyard. The three-storey centre section was the Market Hall, Sir William de Clopton's gift to the town in 1438 and probably cannibalised from the second church (the third, counting Guthrum's) as the present stone building was going up. The two-storey extensions on each side of the Market Hall came in 1451, transforming the building into the Guildhall; the western extension held the **medieval kitchen** where the guildsmens' banquets were prepared.

A medieval guild was a strange mixture of town council, tradesmen's federation, benevolent society, bank, and early trade union, often with a dash of religion and sometimes – as here at Hadleigh – incorporating a school. The Guildhall's Grammar School survived into the 19th cent, and if you look on the wall of the nearby **corn exchange,** built in 1813, you will see marks caused by children sharpening their slate pencils on their way to school.

Deanery Tower. The other contender for the title of most impressive building is the Deanery Tower, which looks like an enormous folly. It was begun in 1495 as the great entrance to the new rectory for the Archdeacon of Suffolk, William Pykenham, who had become rector of Hadleigh in 1472 on the strength of the town's links with the Archbishop of Canterbury. Pykenham had built the almshouses in George Street but he died in 1497 before he could complete the rectory.

Feoffment. Sir William de Clopton's gift of the Market Hall was to be administered by 24 trustees known as the Hadleigh Market Feoffment Charity; gradually they took control of Pykeham's Deanery Tower and almshouses which they *still* run as the Grand Feoffment.

Thomas Gainsborough rises over market day in Sudbury.

71

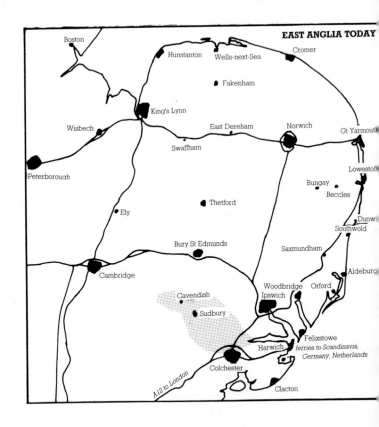

Feoffment? The *Concise Oxford Dictionary* defines the word as 'a mode of conveying freehold estate by formal transfer of possession.'

The Reformation. The 16th-cent Reformation split Hadleigh. The Guildhall, the assets of the five richest guilds, and the church ornaments were confiscated and given to favourites of Henry VIII. A few years later, in the reign of Mary I, Rowland Tayler, Hadleigh's rector and therefore a 'Canterbury Peculiar' in his own right, was burned at the stake.

Under Good Queen Bess (Elizabeth I, 1558-1603), the town recovered its guildhall, but the church treasures were lost forever. Around this time the market for Hadleigh's heavy broadcloth collapsed, and the local weavers failed to develop new textiles. The

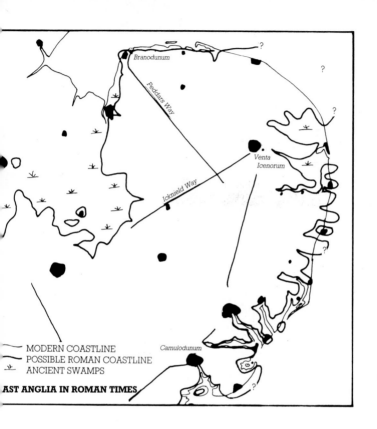

MODERN COASTLINE
POSSIBLE ROMAN COASTLINE
ANCIENT SWAMPS

EAST ANGLIA IN ROMAN TIMES

result was widespread poverty among the labouring classes, which urged the few remaining wealthy families to convert the guildhall into a workhouse.

Authorised Version. Yet the Grammar School part of the guildhall was at its most creative, with its former pupils John Overall and John Boise helping to write the Authorised Version of the Bible, the King James version, in 1611.

High Church. Affairs of the Church had their beginnings in Hadleigh once more, with a group of Oxford intellectuals who met in the Dean's Study in the Deanery Tower to plan the 1833 reformation of church procedure. The planners were known as the **Oxford Movement** and the result was the return of some of the ritual that had been

74 An elegant Queen Anne doorway in Nayland.

abandoned in that other Reformation of the 16th cent; it's now called High Church.

Toppesfield Hall. Sir William de Clopton, who had given the town its Market Hall, lived in the manor house, Toppesfield Hall – pronounce the first E – just over the garden wall from the Guildhall. Sir William had inherited the rights to Hadleigh Market, which Henry III had granted in 1252 to Gilbert de Kyrkeby, then lord of the Manor of Toppesfield. Gilbert or his family built Toppesfield Bridge to allow customers and traders to reach his market from the king's highway, but for the next four centuries the owners of Toppesfield were responsible for maintaining the bridge at their own expense.

John Turner became lord of the manor during Elizabethan times, and records show that the town paid his wife 40 shillings (£2) a year to teach children; as the Grammar School was thriving, historians assume Mrs Turner's pupils formed an early kindergarten.

The Strutt family moved into Toppesfield in the early 17th cent, with Sir Denner Strutt defending Colchester against Cromwell's men in 1648. Strutt was fined for his loyalty to the crown, but on his death in 1661 his name was written in capitals in the Hadleigh Parish Register. The Strutts sold to the Barter-Snows in 1925, and they passed the hall to Hadleigh Council in 1954, when it became the Town Hall. But local government reorganisation in 1974, and the creation of Babergh District Council, meant that Toppesfield was surplus to requirement; the town council had moved back to the Guildhall.

Tourist office. Ten years later the East Anglian Tourist Board took Toppesfield for its headquarters, and it now doubles as the Hadleigh Tourist Office, open Mon-Fri 0900-1715 year round; ✆0473.822922.

Town centre treasures. Almost all of Hadleigh's historic treasures are in this tight cluster of buildings around the church, but stroll down Angel Street and George Street for a selection of half-timbered houses. For a glance at another aspect of history, take Railway Walk south out of town. A branch line of the railway came from Bentley in 1847 but passenger traffic never paid its way and ceased in 1932; the line closed for goods traffic in 1965.

ATTRACTIONS. The annual **Hadleigh Show** is held in mid May on Holbecks Park; the nearby house called **Holbecks,** home of Sir Joshua and Lady Rowley, opens its gardens in July.

HADLEIGH SHOPS. Hadleigh is a small town but it has a very good shopping centre for general needs, lacking only the major chain stores – but there's a large Tesco on the edge of town. **Pubs:** Cheers, The Cock, Eight Bells, Falcon, George, King's Arms, King's Head, The Ram, Wheatsheaf, and White Hart.

OUT OF TOWN

North-west lies the pretty village of **Kersey,** noted for the ford in the middle of the main street and consequently popular with coach tours; this is the home of thriller-writer Hammond Innes.

Corn Craft. The twin villages of **Monks Eleigh** and **Brent Eleigh,** with their wealth of Tudor houses, take their name from the Illeigh family, the first to hold the manorial rights. East of Monks Eleigh on the A1141 is Corn Craft, where the Gage family began re-creating bygone rural ways in 1977. Roy and Winifred grow flowers for cutting and for drying on their 70 acres (28ha), and their shop sells dried flower arrangements, home-made preserves, pottery, corn dollies, and cream teas.

They explain that the craft of making **corn dollies** began around 3,000BC with Demeter, the Greek goddess of agriculture, Ceres being her Roman counterpart. The farmers believed the goddess to be present in the last sheaf of wheat, and threshing it would kill her. The goddess, in later pagan times the 'corn spirit,' was kept alive overwinter in a figure made from cornstalks which was returned to the fields in the spring. Despite Christianity coming to Britain the corn dolly persisted, and the Church incorporated the 'last sheaf' in the harvest festival. Corn Craft, ✆0449.740456, is open daily 1000-1700, free.

The common at **Aldham** has a memorial to Rowland Tayler, Hadleigh's rector who was burned at the stake; away to the east, near Ipswich, is **Hintlesham,** whose 16th-cent hall was the home of the restauranteur Robert Carrier but is now a prestigious hotel and restaurant. **Raydon** is a tiny village which has the concrete runways of a World War Two airfield, and extensive woodland – some of it owned by Hammond Innes.

England's oldest house? But your biggest surprise may come at **Little Wenham,** near the A12. The heart of the village – the church, castle and manor – is at the end of a mile-long unmade road. St Lawrence's Church is redundant and locked (a map at the door tells you where to borrow the keys), and you'll seldom see any activity in the farm buildings around although a medieval brick barn opposite has a new tile roof. The castle is really **Little Wenham Hall,** a fortified manor from the 12th cent and now claimed to be the oldest house in England. Respect the large *private* notices, but there's a footpath which gives a good view of a 16th-cent manor across its moat; the building is in such good condition one wonders why it's empty. The church is open for one service a year, the hall on rare and random dates and visitors are discouraged.

5: SMOOTH STREAM

Bures and about

THE RIVER STOUR at Bures and towards Sudbury is a pleasant, placid stream meandering gently through its picturesque but not spectacular valley, for most of its length with the county boundary on its right bank. But come in a wet winter and you will see the watermeadows flooded and the river a half-mile-wide brown torrent.

BURES

St. Edmund. Bures is a small village sitting astride the river, dabbling its feet in both counties. Nothing seems to happen here nowadays but, on Christmas Day 855, Edmund was crowned King of East Anglia in the parish. Legend claims that he was born at Nuremberg and adopted by Offa, the man who built the dyke between England and Wales. The Danes captured him in 870 and, when he refused to renounce Christianity, beheaded him at Hoxne, but some stories claim he was used for archery practice. In the 9th cent his bones were taken to Bury which later changed its name to Bury St Edmunds in honour of the man known as Edmund – Saint, King and Martyr.

St Mary the Virgin. Despite this strong link with a local saint, Bures's squat-towered church is dedicated to St Mary the Virgin. Standing in Suffolk, it serves the parish of Bures St Mary as well as the Essex parish of Bures Hamlet. The 14th-cent church with later additions had a wooden-framed spire on top of its tower until a lightning strike in 1733 set fire to it; the heat was so intense that five of the six bells melted. The survivor has now been joined by seven others, the last two in 1951, giving Bures one of the best peals in Suffolk.

Waldegraves. The Waldegrave family has its tombs in the church, in recognition of numerous gifts to the building down the ages, including the vestry roof, the font, a side chapel, the Waldegrave Chapel, and part of the tower, with only the latter two surviving. Wall plaques show that Sir Richard Waldegrave, the first Speaker of the House of Commons, came from Walgrave in Northants and married

Lady Joan de Bures, the widow of Sir Robert de Bures. Other Waldegraves are at Lawford and Borley.

And in a vault below the sanctuary lie the remains of Mary Constable, John's aunt.

The origins of the village's name are uncertain. The Domesday record calls it *Bura* and *Bure,* and the name could have come over from Normandy. Or it may be Old English *bur,* a cottage or bower, or the Celtic word for boundary. In the 13th cent it was Bures Nostre Dame, changing to Bures Seinte Marie a century later.

Chapel Barn. A mile (1.6km) north-east of the church is the Chapel of St Stephen, dedicated to the saint on his special day in 1218 by another Stephen, Archbishop Langton of Canterbury – yet believed to be built on the spot where Edmund was crowned in 855. It holds effigies of the 5th, 8th and 11th earls of Oxford (see East Bergholt, Earls Colne and Castle Hedingham) and after the 16th-cent Reformation it was used as a cattleshed, farm cottage, and a 'pesthouse' during the 1739 outbreak of smallpox. It also saw use as a barn, hence the popular name of the Chapel Barn, and it was reconsecrated in the 1930s.

SHOPS IN BURES. General stores and Post Office stores. **Pubs:** Eight Bells, Three Horseshoes.

Assington. St Edmunds Lane leads to Assington, where St Edmund's Church is believed to stand on the site of the last battle between Saxons and Danes; the neighbouring hall was originally a priests' house whose occupants prayed for the souls of those who died in the battle. The pub is the Shoulder of Mutton.

Mount Bures. The tiny village of Mount Bures, south-west of Bures itself, sits on a scenic spur of land with the Stour to the north and Cambridge Brook to the west. St John the Baptist's church, beside the manor house, is built of unbroken flints, with a squat tower carrying a stumpy spire which looks like a funny hat. The small church has a big plaque to Philip Gurdon, rector, and another to the Rev John Gurdon, his son, who died 1799 aged 42. John shares his tomb with his wife Elizabeth who died five years later, aged 61, the difference of 14 years in that direction being unusual for the times. A small plaque remembers John Collins, Canon of St Paul's Cathedral until 1982, who lived here for 12 years.

The B1508, formerly the A133, leads comfortably north to Sudbury along the Suffolk bank, but the corresponding road on the Essex side is hilly and narrow. Lamarsh is tiny, its only pub the Red Lion, and Henny Street is even smaller, its pub being the Swan. South of Henny Street a picturesque but modern footbridge arches across the river – but don't come here for fishing. As along most of the Stour, fishing rights are reserved for club members.

The Colne valley. Earls Colne is a small town making its living from iron and steel. Hunt makes lorry jacks, Crittall makes steel windows and now aluminium ones as well, and elsewhere you could buy tortoise stoves, the efficient but ugly heaters used in Nissen huts during the war. The earls? They were the de Veres, earls of Oxford (see Bures), and 13 of them are buried in the priory.

Wakes Colne and its twin village Chappel have the impressive Chappel Viaduct on the Network Southeast line to Sudbury. Chappel and Wakes Colne station is open to normal passengers, but the old sidings and sheds now form the **Chappel and Wakes Colne Railway Museum,** open daily 1000-1700, admission around £1.50. On special days the museum gets steam up in its tank locomotive and the entrance fee increases. ✆0206.242524.

Further west, **Halstead** had a mix of brass and iron industries along with silk and crêpe and, more recently, Courtaulds had a large textile factory here. The 15th-cent Church of St Andrew is at the top of the steep main street, with tombs of the Bourchier family; descendants of the clan included Lord Berners who was Governor of Calais.

A stretch of the **Colne Valley Railway** has been relaid at **Castle Hedingham** to provide track for a private-enterprise tourist attraction featuring several working locomotives, an assortment of rolling stock, and several items of fixed stock relocated from other sites. Have a five-course Egon-Ronay-recommended meal in the Pullman dining car, hire a train for your party – or just come and look. Open daily Mar-Dec 1100-1700 or dusk if earlier; £1.50 adults. Several steam days a year. ✆0787.61174.

Hedingham Castle. Further up the Colne valley, the four-storey keep of Hedingham Castle in Castle Hedingham village, is in an excellent state of preservation. This enormous structure, begun in 1140 by Aubrey de Vere, is all that remains of a much larger building which must have drained the economy and the labour force for miles around for several years – it would be a major contract today, when we have power lifts, power tools, and lorries.

The doorway and much interior masonry is a fine example of Norman style, and the banqueting hall has the best Norman arch in England. The bridge over the dry moat is Tudor, built by the 13th Earl of Oxford in 1469. Open daily Apr-Oct, 1000-1700; ✆0787.60261.

The next village up the valley, **Great Yeldham,** has the trunk and lower branches of an ancient oak at the side of the main road, and from here a few cross-country miles take us to Clare in Suffolk, where our journeys end.

Golfers at Newton Green tee off beside a main road.

Crossing the Brett at Higham.

6: GAINSBOROUGH'S BIRTHRIGHT

Sudbury and Borley

YOU CANNOT SPEND LONG IN SUDBURY without realising that this is the birthplace of Thomas Gainsborough, considered to be Britain's finest portrait painter.

Thomas Gainsborough. Gainsborough's date of birth is not known, but he was born in what is now Gainsborough's House Museum and was baptised on 14 May 1727. The family was wealthy, Gainsborough senior having been apprenticed to a saymaker ('say' is the old name for serge) and so found himself in a commanding position in the country's richest industry; at one time he owned 11 houses and 22 acres in North St, Sudbury. He married twice, producing three sons and two daughters.

Thomas Gainsborough, like Constable later, had painting as his sole ambition, although he enjoyed music and played several instruments. Like Constable, he preferred to paint landscapes, but as there was even less market for them in the mid-18th cent than there was a generation later, he sensibly concentrated on portraits – 'face painting' as he called it.

He went to London in 1740 to stay with a family friend while he became a pupil of the French engraver Hubert Gravelot. His earliest jobs included restoring, painting small landscapes and selling them for a few shillings, and modelling in clay, but he also developed a taste for alcohol and women.

Marriage. His marriage, on 15 July 1746, caused a minor scandal as he chose Margaret Burr who proudly claimed to be the illegitimate daughter of a prince, from whom she had a settlement of £200 a year for life: years later it was revealed that she was the daughter of the Duke of Beaufort. Did Gainsborough marry purely for love, or did this guaranteed income have a bearing on his proposal? The wedding was held in a chapel noted for eloping couples, which added to the speculation.

Two years later the couple was back in Sudbury, with Thomas struggling to make a living, even at face-painting. He filled in time

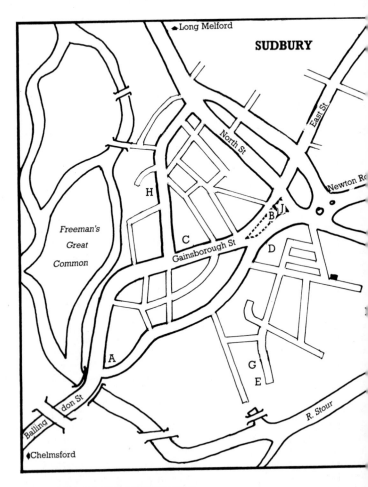

KEY TO SUDBURY MAP

A All Saints Church
B Gainsborough Statue
C Gainsborough's House Museum
D Library
E Quay Theatre

F Rail station
G River Stour Trust
H St Gregory's Church
J St Peter's Church

with a few landscapes and the occasional portrait-landscape composite, but eventually borrowed £400 on the strength of his wife's annuity.

Ipswich. Realising that Sudbury could not support an unknown portrait painter, he moved in 1752 to Ipswich, which then had a population of 11,000, including a number of wealthy merchants who needed a portrait to enhance their social status. From his house in Foundation Street – the name described all that remained of Cardinal Wolsey's Ipswich College – Gainsborough gradually gained acceptance; by 1753 he was painting Admiral Edward Vernon, Ipswich MP and the man who gave 'grog' to the navy (see *Discover the Suffolk Coast*), his fees at that time being 5 guineas (£5.25) for a head and 15gns (£15.75) for a half-body. In February 1755 the Duke of Bedford commissioned him at 21gns (£22.05), and came back for more – but still Gainsborough had to borrow £200.

Two years later he was beginning to manage without Margaret's income, so in 1758 he went to the Midlands searching for commissions, but was back home again by January 1759, and again in debt.

Sold up. On 20 October of that year the *Ipswich Journal* announced:

> To be sold, the 22nd & 23rd inst. All the HOUSEHOLD
> GOODS of Mr THOMAS GAINSBOROUGH with some PIC-
> TURES and original DRAWINGS in the Landskip [landscape]
> way. The house to be let immediately.

The Gainsboroughs went to Bath early in 1760, and Thomas had begun to make a lasting impression on the art world before the year was out; he had commissions which took him to Longleat and Badminton, and in 1761 he was making several visits to London, where alcohol and women again diverted his interests; he fell ill, prompting the *Bath Journal* to print his obituary quickly followed by an apology.

King George III granted a charter of incorporation in January 1765 to the Society of Arts of Great Britain, to which Gainsborough was admitted as Fellow on 11 March; it was the beginning of the Royal Academy which, in April 1769, exhibited its first Gainsborough.

Fame and social acceptance were now within grasp – but the following month Thomas's mother died, and was buried in the Independent Meeting House in Sudbury.

The Gainsborough's House museum has a copy of a letter from the artist to the Earl of Dartmoor, dated 18 April 1771, which shows his continued dislike of portraiture:

My Lord. Here it is then – Nothing can be more absurd than the foolish custom of Painters dressing people like Scaramouches, and expecting the likeness to appear; had a picture Voice, Action, &c to make itself known, as Actors have upon the stage, no disguise would be sufficient to conceal a person...

Royal rumpus. Gainsborough continued to strengthen his reputation so that by 1784 he was painting the portrait of Admiral Rodney who had recently taken supplies to Gibraltar during its Great Siege; soon Thomas was painting George III and Queen Charlotte at Windsor. Gainsborough then told the Royal Academy how to hang his pictures, with the result that the academy rejected his entire work. When the position of principal Portrait Painter to the king became vacant soon after, Gainsborough assumed he would get the post, but as he was in disagreement with the king's own academy and Joshua Reynolds was its president, Reynolds was appointed.

Despite that setback, Gainsborough was at the height of his fame and prosperity, selling 'Fancy-Pictures' and even 'Landskips,' the former at 40gns a head, 80gns half-length and 160gns for a full portrait – but Reynolds was charging more.

Prophesy of death. Then early in 1787 when Gainsborough and the playwright Richard Sheridan were dining together, the artist prophesied his own death in the near future. The portrait of the Duke of Norfolk, finished in the spring of 1788, was Gainsborough's last major work; he caught a chill sitting in Westminster Hall at the trial of Warren Hastings at which Sheridan was appearing for the prosecution, and wrote:

My swelled Neck is got very painful indeed...God only knows what is for me, but hope is the Pallat Colors (sic) we all paint with in sickness...I am so childish that I could make a Kite...or built little Ships.

By mid-June the surgeons had diagnosed cancer, and Gainsborough died at 0200 on 3 August with the words: "We are all going to heaven, and van Dyke is of the party." He was buried in Kew Churchyard.

For a fuller account read *Thomas Gainsborough* by Jack Lindsay, Granada, 1981.

SUDBURY

Gainsborough's House. In the 1950s a group of people bought 46 Gainsborough St in Sudbury (the postcode is CO10 6EU, ✆0787.72958) to restore it and convert it into a museum. The two 15th-cent cottages, with a common Georgian front built by Gainsborough's father in 1725, are therefore the property of a charitable trust, the Gainsborough's House Society, with an entrance fee of £1.50; open Easter Saturday to end of September, Tues-Sat 1000-1700, Sun 1400-1700; rest of the year closing at 1600. Open Mon on bank holidays only, 1400-1700.

The building itself is full of character, with leaning doorways, creaking floors, a steep staircase – not suitable for ♿ visitors although several tour the ground floor. One of the cottages had been the Black Horse Inn and either may have been a mill, for Gainsborough commented: "pimply-nosed Rembrandt and I were both born in a mill." So, of course, were Constable and Munnings.

A precious few of Gainsborough's paintings are on view here, their value on the open market making it extremely difficult for the society to buy. The society owns several canvases, including *Portrait of a Boy*, but most Gainsborough paintings on display here are on short-term loan from major galleries, museums, and private collectors; the largest display of Gainsboroughs and Constables outside London is at Christchurch Mansion, Ipswich, If you'd like to help the society you can become a Friend of the Development Trust for £8 a year, £13 joint membership.

Gainsborough's House also holds a series of unrelated art exhibitions such as papermaking, lino cuts, modern painting – and there is a print room on view using ancient machinery. And when you've seen it all, relax for a while in the garden at the rear.

There's no **car parking** space near the house any longer; I suggest you park near the Solar supermarket (see map) and explore all of Sudbury town centre on foot.

SUDBURY IN HISTORY

Suth-burgh was the 'fortified town of the south' to the Angles. The Normans recorded in 1086 that it had 63 *burghers*, later to be known as 'freemen.' Richard de Clare gave Sudbury freemen their first privilege in the 13th cent, a gift of land by the river.

Fire buckets. In 1505, the weaver William Slater paid a 'fine' to

Fen Street, Nayland; the houses are in Suffolk, the road in Essex.

become a freeman, and a decree in 1576 stated *every Occupier [such as] Grocer, Draper, Haberdasher...shall pay foreign Fyne for the first yere [year] 13s 4d [66.5p] and so every Yere till he be made a Freeman...*' Later, sons of Sudbury's freemen could become freemen themselves at the age of 21, by presenting the mayor with two fire-buckets, but after the Corporation's sale of 260 buckets in 1813, the custom ceased.

In the late 19th cent an Act of Parliament allowed the borough to appoint honorary freemen, which allowed Brigadier-General Charles Dawes to receive the honour in the 1950s. He had been Vice-President to Herbert Hoover from 1925 to '29 and US ambassador to the United Kingdom immediately after. You may have guessed his ancestors came from Sudbury.

Market. Sudbury had a market before the Norman Conquest, the lord of the manor taking the profit, and it still has a busy market now – on Thursday, when parking is the most difficult. A document from Roger Mortimer, Earl of March, dated 1397, gave Sudbury's Mayor and bailiffs the right to elect two sergeants to carry the mace. This proves that the town already had a mayor – and it still has one today.

Assizes. At the end of a trial at the local assizes in December 1791 when the jury couldn't agree on a verdict its members were locked up 'without fire and candle' in a first-floor room at the Old Moot Hall. They all agreed it was cold, so they knotted their neckerchiefs to make a rope, and escaped through the window. Next day the embarrassed mayor released the prisoner and decided not to talk of the escaping jurors – so who recorded the story?

Nine years earlier Sarah Green, convicted of stealing clothing worth 9d (4p), was put in an open cart and 'publicly whipt' on her naked back. In the early 17th cent Martin and George Warren were convicted of 'killing a bull not being baited' – contrary to the law, the bull had *not* been worried by dogs before the slaughter – but in 1842 people were fined £5 for bull-baiting at Lavenham.

Assize records also show that in Tudor times beggars needed a licence from the magistrate. Those caught begging illegally were branded on first conviction, enslaved on second, and executed on third conviction.

Priories and college. Sudbury had several priories, among them **St Bartholomew's,** built after 1130 a mile north of town and valued at £10 at its dissolution in 1543. By contrast **Sudbury Priory,** built in 1272 by Baldwin de Shimperling on Friars St, was worth £222 at the dissolution. Its material was re-used to build Ballingdon Hall on the same site, but that was demolished in 1820. Remarkably, in 1381 it had a water supply brought across the river in lead pipes 2in (6cm) in diameter. The **Dominican Priory** in Friars St was destroyed in the dissolution, but the Priory Gate and the hostelry survive, the latter as the **Ship and**

Star pub with small rooms and exposed beams.

Simon Theobald, son of 14th-cent Sudbury clothiers, studied at Paris, became Bishop of London in 1361, Archbishop of Canterbury in 1375, and four years later was Lord Chancellor to Richard II. He began **Sudbury College** soon after, but was murdered in the Peasants' Revolt of 1381 protesting at the poll tax. Work continued on the college, and at the dissolution of the monasteries in 1538 it passed undamaged to Henry VIII. Sir Thomas Paston, who wrote the Paston Letters, bought the college in 1544 for £1,280, a fortune, but by 1702 it was the workhouse. It was demolished in 1836.

St Peter's Church. The town centre church of St Peter is, surprisingly, not the main church. It began as a chapel of ease to St Gregory's, with the present building dating from the late 15th cent. William Dowsing was here in January 1643: "We brake down a picture of God the Father, two crucifixes, and pictures of Christ, about 100 in all." Plus the cross from the steeple and angels from the roof.

The vicar of 1859 took the box pews out by night for sale on Market Hill the next day, but parishioners who objected served an injunction on the auctioneer banning the sale. He pocketed the paper saying he'd attend to it after the sale. The church is now redundant and closed, but you might borrow the keys from Steed & Steed at 6 Gainsborough St or the shop at 41 Friar St.

St Gregory's. The main church is St Gregory's, built in the 14th cent on the site where, according to the Anglo-Saxon Chronicle, Bishop

Nayland: St James's church spire, a tall chimney, and a milestone.

Alfwin of Dunwich died in 797. Nigel and Sarah Theobald lived beside the church, and the head of their son Simon, the Archbishop of Canterbury murdered by Wat Tyler's mob, is in the vestry. The rest of the archbishop is in the choir of Canterbury Cathedral with a ball of lead for his head.

Henry VII's wife Elizabeth, a descendant of the Clare family, regularly sent a priest on pilgrimage to St Mary's Chapel (it's now called St Anne's) as it contained the statue of Our Lady of Sudbury. It's not here now, nor are the 'ten mighty great Angels in Glass,' for William Dowsing smashed most of the stained glass windows.

Sudbury camel. Thomas Carter left a strange tombstone in the chapel. It reads in translation from Latin: *on the day Thomas Carter breathed his last, a Sudbury camel passed through the eye of a needle. If you are wealthy, go and do likewise.*

All Saints'. All Saints', on Church St near Ballingdon Bridge, was established when the first records appear in the 12th cent. The church was in the patronage of St Albans Abbey until it was demolished in 1539, yet its priest of 1381 was so involved with the Peasants' Revolt that he was executed. Dowsing destroyed 'about 20 superstitious pictures' and ripped up 30 brasses in January 1643, and in the Dutch War of 1672-'74, prisoners kept in the church damaged it severely.

Other buildings. Sudbury's **Corn Exchange,** now the town library on Market Hill, has kept its Classical pillars, and **Salter's Hall** is a good example of 15th-cent building. Look at the door of the **Bull Inn** by Ballingdon Bridge for the carved date 1693.

Quay Theatre. An 18th-cent granary by the riverside is now the Quay Theatre, home of the Sudbury Dramatic Society and fellow groups interested in light opera, jazz, and cottage crafts: they all display their talents in the theatre. ✆0787.74745; ♿.

More details are in *History of Sudbury* by C.G. Grimwood and S.A. Kay, self-published 1952.

TOURIST OFFICE. The tourist office is in a large caravan near the railway station, open Mon-Fri 0900-1700; ✆0787.881320. **Parking:** Ample free parking around the tourist caravan and the Solar supermarket, some with a three-hour limit.

SHOPS. Sudbury is a good shopping centre, with many nationally-known names represented. **Pubs:** Anchor, Angel, Bear, Black Boy, Black Horse, Boathouse, Christopher, Four Swans, Great Eastern, Horn, Horse & Groom, Jades, Maldon Grey, Mill, Old Red Cow, Plough, Prince of Wales, Royal Oak, Ship & Star, Spread Eagle, Wagon & Horses, Waterman's Arms, White Horse.

GOLF. There's an 18-hole roadside course at Newton Green. Villagers have 'commoners rights;' others pay a greens fee.

BORLEY

Drive three miles north-east of Sudbury, and you are in a different world altogether. The old rectory in the tiny village of Borley was alleged to be the most haunted house in England – and there are still strange happenings in the village after dark. Don't get involved; the police wouldn't welcome your presence by night.

Borley has a presentable church and a scattering of houses and bungalows, but no pub, no shop, no post office, no school, and no obvious centre.

Borley Rectory. In 1863 the Rev H. D. Bull built a rectory roughly opposite the church, to hold his large family, but he either defied the legend of the Nun's Walk or he didn't know about it.

The ghost of the nun, Marie Lairre, had long walked the village lanes, and in particular trod the route across open fields, a route which came to be known locally as the Nun's Walk. Legend claimed that Marie had been bricked up alive for having a love affair with a Borley monk, but another version was that she had been murdered by a member of the Waldegrave family, which held the lordship of the manor in the 16th cent: see Lawford and Bures.

Now, Marie Lairre objected to the rectory blocking her path, and she would often gaze at the rector through the window of his study. He blocked up the window and thereafter ignored the nun.

Phantom coach. Mr Bull's son Harry succeeded him as rector and held the office until 1927, despite increased visits from Marie, who now manifested in daylight as well and was seen by the postman and other people in the village. Marie's occasional companion, a phantom coach drawn by four headless horses – a common ingredient in East Anglian ghost stories – now drove right through the rectory several times, scaring the servants away.

In 1927 the new incumbent, Eric Smith, told his story to the *Daily Mirror*, which sent the well-known psychic investigator Harry Price down to Borley.

Price had a bonanza. The spirits put on a major show for him, throwing a candlestick at his head, snatching keys from the keyholes, and tapping out messages on the walls. Borley Rectory became infamous overnight.

'Please get help.' Mr Smith resigned, the new rector being Lionel Foyster who moved in with his wife Marianne. Marianne appeared to attract the spirits, for a series of pencilled messages appeared on the rectory walls asking her for help. Many were overwritten and illegible, but among the recognisable words were *light...mass.. .candles...please get help.*

The Foysters moved out in fear, leaving the rectory empty. Harry Price came back in 1937, leasing it for a year and appealing for psychic investigators to join him. Among the many replies was one from Professor C. E. M. Joad who later made a name for himself on BBC radio's *Brains Trust.*

On one particular night, Price and Joad marked the site of all movable objects with chalk rings, placed thermometers around to record any temperature drop, then locked all the rooms. The ghosts performed, throwing candlesticks and holding bricks motionless in the air long enough to be photographed. In a later séance, Marie Lairre identified herself, claiming to have been strangled on 17 May 1667 and then buried beside the Nun's Walk. At another séance on 27 March 1938, a spirit which called itself Sunex Amores warned that the rectory would burn down that night, the fire starting 'over the hall.'

Fire. It didn't. Price left soon after, and a Captain Gregson bought the lease. The spirits were just as active, driving away the captain's dogs, then on 27 February 1939, 11 months to the night after the warning, an oil lamp in a room over the hall fell – or was thrown – to the floor, and the prophesy of fire was fulfilled, leaving only the brick shell of the rectory.

And still the ghost of Marie Lairre walked, this time even appearing at the first floor window holes of the gaunt ruin, standing on floors that no longer existed. Harry Price came back in 1943, found the bones of a young woman buried beneath the cellar floor, and claimed them to be those of the strangled nun. Although they were buried in a consecrated cemetery which some people believe quietens the wandering spirits, legend still claims that the ghost of Marie Lairre infrequently comes back to stroll the site of the rectory and wander in the churchyard.

Borley Rectory today. Today nothing at all remains of the rectory, and a new bungalow called Crosslands stands on the site; the owner sells plants at the gate to raise funds for a church in Sudbury.

Borley Church, whose dedication is unknown, is almost permanently locked except on Sundays – even the car park is chained off – and you'll find it very difficult to locate anybody who has a key, so you'll have to accept unverified the statement that the tomb of Sir Edward Waldegrave, who died in 1561, is the most prominent feature inside.

No peace. Borley Rectory is gone, but peace has not come to the village. Youths on motor-cycles have smashed headstones among the beautifully-sculpted yews in the churchyard, and others have tried to break down the church door at dead of night. Even now, on several nights a week throughout the year, groups of people arrive by car or motor-cycle after sunset and leave again in the early hours. The villagers stay behind locked doors and don't ask whether the visitors are ordinary people hoping to see the ghost of Marie Lairre tread the ruins of Borley Rectory – or whether there is black magic afoot.

7: BABBLING BROOK

Long Melford to Clare, with Lavenham

THIS UPPER COURSE of the River Stour flows past three villages which a generous person might call towns, but it flows through a large part of England's history and influences the stories of Wales and Ireland as well.

Wool later played a major part in that story and gave us the charm of Long Melford and the unique beauty of Lavenham sitting beside the Brett, a tributary of the Stour.

LONG MELFORD

Long Melford's main road, Hall St and Little St Mary's St, is a mile (1.6km) from end to end, most of it lined with 18th and 19th cent shops and houses, with occasional Tudor property. Luckily those original builders allowed for a roadway around 200ft (60m) wide. Melford made its fortune in the wool trade then, like Glemsford, moved to other staples, employing 170 people in weaving coconut fibre and 400 in horsehair, the last few of them working into the 1960s, but today its main business is centred around the 21 antiques shops.

Much of the village's history is bound up in the church and the stately homes, Kentwell Hall and Melford Hall, but Bridge House, on the south of the 14-acre (5.5ha) green, was home of poet Edmund Blunden.

The Bull Hotel. The village's most important hostelry is the Bull Hotel, built around 1450 for a wool merchant and converted to an inn during Henry VIII's dissolution of the monasteries. In 1648 Richard Evered, a wealthy yeoman, was murdered in the hall, and his murderer executed – but the ghost of one of them, if not both, has haunted the hotel since, with furniture occasionally moved and chills settling in the dining room. The carved beams in the ceiling of the drawing room are probably the best in Suffolk, with the 10in (27cm) wide main beam having a carving of the green man (see Clare).

The Bull was the main posting house in Long Melford for London coaches bound for Bury St Edmunds and Norwich. The beautiful timberwork on the front was discovered in 1935 when the Georgian brickwork was removed, but nobody has yet discovered the secret room which is supposed to be on the first floor.

Holy Trinity Church. Long Melford's church has one of the best sites in the eastern counties, commanding the view of the village to the south and, with a nave and chancel stretching 150ft (45m), is among the largest in the county.

A Roman temple probably stood on the spot, and a church was certainly here by 1050, but the present church, financed by wool, was completed in 1484 with the lady chapel in 1496. Lightning destroyed the tower around 1710, the brick replacement of 1725 being encased in the present tower, built in 1903 for Queen Victoria's Jubilee. Legend claims that a medieval window showing Elizabeth Talbot, Duchess of Norfolk, was John Tenniel's model for the Duchess in *Alice in Wonderland*. The best-known window is a tiny roundel over the door showing three rabbits each with two ears, yet with only three ears showing; this signifies the Trinity.

The Kentwell Aisle, reserved for residents of Kentwell Hall, has a bas-relief of the Adoration of the Magi which predates the church by about 150 years. The Cordell tomb, in front of the altar, is in memory of Sir William Cordell, Speaker of the House of Commons, Master of the Rolls, and rebuilder of Melford Hall in the time of Elizabeth I.

Holy Trinity Church escaped William Dowsing's attentions in 1643, probably because a gang of '3,000 of the scum of Colchester' plundered Melford Hall the previous year and probably went on to rob the church as well.

GARDENS OPEN. Conduit House and Ely House, on the same Sunday in July with a combined ticket.

LONG MELFORD SHOPS, excluding the antiques: butcher, baker, general store, hardware, bookshop, patisserie, pharmacy, lingerie, saddlery, Post Office. **Pubs:** Cock and Bell, Crown Inn, George and Dragon, Swan. **Restaurants:** Chimneys, and the Bull Hotel.

KENTWELL HALL

Kentwell Hall is a Tudor mansion built around 1520-'50, but its owners insist it is not a stately home. When Patrick Phillips bought it in 1971 it had been neglected for years, so what you see is a beautiful 16th-cent family home slowly being restored, with the act of restoration more important than the completion, whenever that may be.

Ownership of the manor of Kentwell is recorded back to 1040 without interruption, and in Domesday, 1086, it was valued at £4, double its worth in Edward the Confessor's reign when it was known as Kanewella, the *wella* being a cluster of springs. The 11th cent owners followed tradition by naming themselves from the manor, but

The Tudor Rose Courtyard at Kentwell Hall.

by 1250 Henry III owned the estate, granting it to his half-brother Sir William de Valence; records of 1287 give the area as 440 acres (178ha). Sir William Clopton inherited the manor in 1403, 12 years before going to fight at Agincourt. His son John, several times sheriff of Norfolk and Suffolk, was a Lancastrian who quickly changed allegiance when his friends were executed for treason.

Princes in the Tower. John was to become a Knight of the Bath at the coronation of 12-year-old Edward V, but the prince was imprisoned in the Tower of London and allegedly murdered by his uncle who became Richard III. John Clopton, however, built Long Melford Church and probably the first Kentwell Hall, though only the Moat House remains.

John and William. John's son, another William, continued with the building between 1497 and 1530, his years of ownership of the manor. He made his reputation in 1497 by opposing Lambert Simnel, impersonating the Earl of Warwick, on Simnel's attempted invasion of England; and in 1502 he was licensed to keep his hat on in the king's presence. William's son, another John, owned the hall from 1530 to '41 but did little; *his* son, not surprisingly called William, continued working on the hall for the next 21 years and was undoubtedly the builder of much of the shell visible today. This William had a large family and a wealthy mother, giving him the motive and the means to create an extensive mansion.

By now, Kentwell Hall was essentially complete. Thomas Clopton, owner 1588-'96, brought his wife Mary to the mansion; she was the daughter of Sir William Waldegrave, whose name occurs elsewhere in this book. Then in 1632 ownership passed to Sir Simons d'Ewes through marriage to Anne, the last of the Cloptons, who was the Member of Parliament for Sudbury until being expelled in 1648. His diary of Parliamentary happenings was the contemporary equivalent of Hansard. The D'Arcy family of St Osyth Priory near Clacton-on-Sea came into the scene in 1650, selling in 1676 to Sir Thomas Robinson, a successful lawyer in London's Inner Temple, who planted the avenue of lime trees. He died in 1683 of burns from a fire in his chambers, leaving £10,000 in coin in an iron chest. That was a fortune, for John Moore paid only £21,000 for Kentwell in 1706, inherited from earnings in the East India trade.

Impending ruin. Richard Moore inherited the hall in 1782. A gambler, he built a farmhouse on the estate to hide from his creditors, but he still managed to keep the family tradition of becoming High Sheriff of Suffolk. He tried selling the limes in the avenue to a piano maker, but eventually the burden of debt was too great, and he died in a debtor's prison in 1826.

Later owners did little to the house but added to the estate until in the mid 19th cent it covered 2,000 acres (8 sq km). Moore's successor in title was an absentee landlord, with tenants including Sir John Aird, builder of the first Aswan Dam in Egypt (1906-'15). The last tenant found the upkeep a great burden and on his death in 1969 the estate was put on the market, passing in 1971 to its present owner, Patrick Phillips, lawyer and Queen's Counsel, who brought his new wife Judith here in 1976.

Rare sheep. The Norfolk Horn sheep, which created East Anglia's wool wealth, was down to three rams and five ewes by 1968. The Phillips family now has 120 breeding ewes and is helping to conserve other endangered breeds of domestic animal.

Tudor re-creation. The Tudor way of life is long extinct, but for around three midsummer weeks it is brought back to life at Kentwell as around 200 people dress, talk, think and live their roles as ordinary people of Tudor times. Attendance at a re-creation costs £8 or more but on normal opening days admission is £3 per adult to the house, £2 to the gardens, with concessions. Kentwell is open mid-Mar–mid-Jun, and Oct, Sundays; mid-Jun–Sep, daily, 1200-1700 house, 1200-1800 gardens. Times may vary year to year. ☎0787.310207.

MELFORD HALL

Melford Hall, only a mile away, is owned by the National Trust and is open Mar-Apr and Oct, Sat-Sun and bank hols; May-Sep, Wed, Thur, Sat, Sun, 1400-1730. Adult entry fee is £2.50

Sir William Cordell, a lawyer who became Speaker of the House of

Commons and Master of the Rolls, probably completed the house by 1578 when he entertained Queen Elizabeth here.

The building was originally a hollow square with one side demolished at a later date, but the north wing, destroyed by fire during World War II, has been rebuilt.

The Parliamentarians looted the hall during the Civil War but when the building reverted to the Cordell family, Sir Cordell Firebrace restored and redecorated the place around 1735.

In 1786 Sir Harry Parker bought Melford Hall; the Parkers were a notable seafaring family with Sir Hyde Parker, Sir Harry's father, becoming Vice-Admiral of the Blue. Sir Hyde Parker II, commanding the British fleet at the Battle of Copenhagen in April 1801, signalled the recall, but a subordinate captain, Horatio Nelson, put his telescope to his blind eye and denied seeing the signal. And so the British won the battle.

Much restored in 1847, the hall has a good collection of pictures, furniture, and porcelain – including some items that the vice-admiral seized in 1762 from the captured Spanish galleon *Santísima Trinidad*, bearing gifts from the Emperor of China.

AROUND LONG MELFORD

Glemsford. The little-visited village of Glemsford, overlooking the River Glem but certainly not close enough to ford it, was involved in

The Stour at Bures is a really smooth stream.

the wool trade but changed direction at the end of the 19th cent by diversifying into other fibres including silk, flax, horsehair and coconut. The latter three have faded away but Glemsford still manufactures silk yarn, some of which went into the Queen's Coronation robe, the Prince of Wales's investiture cloak, and the wedding dresses of Princess Anne and the Princess of Wales.

Some authorities claim Glemsford lacks character; certainly it has a large modern housing estate that detracts from its appearance. The small parish church is usually locked, and the pubs are the Angel, Black Lion, Cherry Tree, and Ye Old Cock.

Up the Glem is another **Boxted,** with a moated hall, the home of the Poley family since the early 15th cent. Sir John Poley, who died in 1638, is shown in the parish church with a golden frog hanging from an ear, an award given by King Christian of Denmark. Due east, accessible through Hartest village, is **Gifford's Hall,** a working farm open to the public and not to be confused with the Gifford Hall near Stoke-by-Nayland. John and Carol Kemp have 33 acres (13ha) on which they grow grapes, flowers for cutting, and vegetables for kitchen and shop. Everything is grown without artificial fertilizers and pesticides, so the meadows are as full of flowers as they were generations ago. Open mid-Apr-Oct daily 1200-1800; ✆0284.830464; admission £1.75 adults.

Foxearth. Across the Stour in Essex is Foxearth, with Huntsman's Farm aptly not far away. The Church of St Peter and St Paul is worth a visit, provided you *walk* down the path from the *western* approach. You'll see a grilled window at the base of the tower, offering a tempting glance into the crypt; then you'll notice the relief carving around the south porch proclaiming *Precious in the sight of the Lord is the death of His Saints* and, squeezed in on the other side, *Be not slothful but followers of those who through faith and patience Merit the Promises.* The highly-decorative painting on the interior walls and ceiling beams is Victorian, and out of keeping with today's taste – and the 1914-'18 war memorial, opposite the porch, is in the form of a Celtic cross.

The church had a Victorian spire as well, but it blew down in 1947.

So who was responsible for the Victoriana here? The Rev John Foster, rector from 1845 until 1892, who used a private fortune on the church then supported a local hospital, built a school in the village, owned a farm, sat on the magistrates' bench, was chairman of the Poor Relief administrators – and builder of the village gas-works!

Bull's Folly. Two miles (3km) west, you can see a tower peering above the treetops. This is the 90-ft (27m) tall Rectory Tower, built in 1862 by the Rev Edward Bull in honour of his parents. The tower is on private land and not accessible as the wooden stairs built around a central pole, are rotting. Mr Bull's church was St Gregory and St

George's in **Pentlow,** on the south bank of the Stour opposite Cavendish.

LAVENHAM

If you would like to step back into the Middle Ages, come to Lavenham. This quiet Suffolk town ranks with Toledo, Bruges, Venice and Hamelin for its charm, character, and unspoilt history, and it is the best-preserved medieval town in the British Isles.

In Saxon times Lavenham was part of the **Babergh Hundred,** an area occupied by 100 freemen and centred on the manors of Overhall and Netherhall, both of which were given to Alberic de Vere, brother-in-law to William the Conqueror. Alberic's grandson **Aubrey de Vere** became first Earl of Oxford in 1103 and built Castle Hedingham. Of the original manors, Babergh Hall and Nether Hall survive near the Waldringfield villages.

Wool. Lavenham began as an agricultural village but by 1257 when Henry III issued its first market charter it was already into commerce. Less than a century later it was involved in the spinning and weaving of cloth, using the skills of the first of many influxes of Flemish weavers – but nobody knows if the Flamands actually settled here.

Dyed in the wool. The town soon specialised in a thick broadloom which was dyed in wood before being woven, from which comes our expression 'dyed in the wool.'

In 1397 Richard II demanded a loan from England's 70 richest towns, in which Lavenham came 52nd, equal with Plymouth and Bath, but just 120 years later, Lavenham was the country's 14th richest town.

Guilds. The wool and weaving trades were strictly controlled by guilds – see Hadleigh – those in Lavenham being Holy Trinity, Our Lady, Corpus Christi, and Saints Peter and Paul. The **Guildhall of Corpus Christi** is the most impressive building in the modern town, dominating Market Place. Completed around 1529 and using far more timber than was necessary, it was redundant by 1547 with the dissolution of the monasteries when the guild was disbanded. Eight years later it was prison to the rector of Hadleigh who was burned at Aldham; in 1596 it became the town hall, and later it saw use as prison again, then a workhouse, almshouse, and wool store.

Today it is a museum, owned by the National Trust, its exhibits explaining the full story of the wool trade with the help of an original loom – but spare a glance at the timberwork, particularly in the ceilings. Open April-Oct daily, 1100-1700; £1.90 adults, photography allowed on request; limited ⅀ access. There's also a tearoom.

Tourist office. The Tourist Information Centre is beside the Guildhall, open daily Easter–mid-Oct, 1000-1645.

The Guildhall of Our Lady was converted into the **Wool Hall** in the late 17th cent, but demolished in 1911 for re-erection on the Ascot estate of the Duchess of Argyll. Several properties vanished in this manner, including the Moot Hall which was rebuilt on Clacton's seafront. But the townspeople blocked the exit so effectively that the duchess agreed to leave the Wool Hall in Lavenham on condition it be used as a convalescent home for wives of railwaymen. It was rebuilt, and now forms part of the **Swan Hotel.**

The Swan is a conglomerate of three houses as well as the rebuilt Wool Hall. The oldest house was in existence in 1425 and while the conversion to an inn is not recorded, it was issuing tokens (coinage usable only on the premises) in 1667. A century later, wool or cloth was stored at first floor level (2nd floor for American readers) around the courtyard, inferring that trade went on wherever possible. Coaches left here three times a week for the two-day round trip to London at a fare of 11s (55p), and by 1830 the Swan was a major coaching inn with stables for 50 horses. The hotel's large dining room

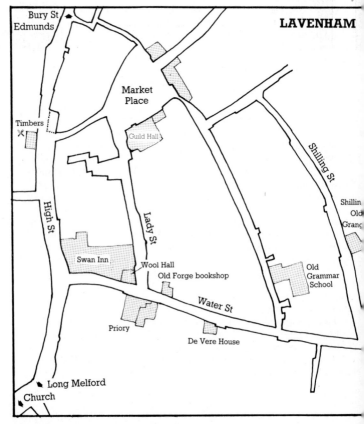

The white-fronted Church of St Mary at Boxford.

is a classic example of medieval timberwork – but it was built in 1965 on the Wool Hall garden, using 400 tons of oak at a cost of £170,000.

487 Group. The Old Bar has a collection of badges left by members of the USAAF 487th Bomb Group who were stationed at **Alpheton,** three miles (2km) north from early 1944 until May 1945, while other American souvenirs are in the Guildhall.

Wool decline. The wool trade went into decline in the 1560s after Dutch refugees introduced cloths of other fibres, the 'new draperies.' Bankruptcies and poverty were rife by 1630, and Lavenham failed to find another industry to restore its affluence – which is why the original houses were neither demolished nor updated, but merely had plaster fronts added. Slight recovery came from spinning, which prevented the town decaying entirely, and this gave way to weaving horsehair which lasted until 1930 and the phasing out of horses on the land.

Only in this century has there been a move to conserve Lavenham's heritage, with most of the plaster fronts being removed to reveal the medieval timberwork.

The Priory. Not every building escaped undamaged. The Priory on Water St, originally a 14th-cent monastery for the Benedictine order, later a cloth merchant's home and an Elizabethan rectory, was dilapidated when Alan and Gwenneth Casey rescued it in the 1980s and began a major restoration job. Seven rooms of the priory are now open to the public daily, Easter-Oct 31, 1030-1730 for £2.

✆0787.247417. There's also a restaurant (closed Fri), herb garden and gift shop.

Other buildings. A selection of other houses of interest must include **Little Hall** in Market Place, now a museum of furniture and art, open Easter-Oct, Wed, Thur, Sat, Sun, bank holidays, 1430-1800 or by appointment, for £1. ✆0787.247179 and its neighbour **The Great House,** the hotel and restaurant behind the market cross of 1502 (ignore the 1725 carved on the shaft), which retains its Georgian façade. Both properties were the home of poet Stephen Spender in the 1950s.

The home of John Shilling in the 15th cent is now **Shilling Old Grange,** where Jane Taylor wrote the nursery rhyme *Twinkle, Twinkle, Little Star,* and the **Grammar School** in Barn Street had an unhappy John Constable for a pupil. Back in Water Street the **de Vere House** was rebuilt in the 1920s but the family symbols of the star and boar are the originals.

Sugar-beet. After studying the workshops of medieval craftsmen, consider that the town today has a busy printing and publishing business, the Lavenham Press, and a large factory making lipstick and other cosmetics on the site of the old railway station where England's first sugar-beet factory once stood.

Lavenham Church. The de Vere family, who held the manor of Lavenham for 500 years, joined the Spryng family in rebuilding the Church of Saints Peter and Paul, completed in 1525, two years after

Detail on the Guildhall at Lavenham.

Thomas Spryng died; his tomb is in the parclose (timber enclosure) in the nave with the heraldic arms of the de Veres. The Late Perpendicular church is similar in size and majesty to that of Long Melford, and also stands at the edge of town. The nave is 191ft (58m) long by 68ft (20m) wide and the tower is 141ft (43m) high, its completion financed by a £200 bequest in Spryng's will. Puritan desire for simplicity has removed the 20 or more brasses, and the box pews went in Victorian times.

Bells. The church's tenor bell, cast in 1625, has been called 'the finest-toned bell in England,' and if you plan your visit to the Swan Hotel's Old Bar you may hear the ringers practising on handbells.

LAVENHAM SHOPS: florists, greencrocer, grocers, confectionery, bookshops, chinaware, butcher, pharmacy, art gallery, baker, Post Office, Sue Ryder shop, tearooms. **Pubs:** Angel, Cock, Greyhound, Swan. **Restaurant:** Timbers.

CAVENDISH

Sue Ryder Foundation. A large group of buildings on the south side of Cavendish's main street holds the headquarters of the Sue Ryder Foundation, where Lady Ryder and her husband Group Captain Lord Leonard Cheshire live in a small flat.

Sue Ryder was born in Leeds in July 1923 into a comfortable family that had a second home at Thurlow in Suffolk. As a child she encountered the terrible poverty of the labouring classes in the industrial north, then in the early days of World War Two she joined the Special Operations Executive to help arrange the dropping of spies and saboteurs in occupied Europe, particularly Poland, coming into contact at second-hand with much of the horror and degradation of Nazism and concentration camps. After the war she volunteered to be a relief worker in Poland where she saw the appalling conditions in which people tried to rebuild their lives not knowing that another 40 years of Communist rule awaited them.

Her experience of poverty at home and abroad prepared her for her charitable work in the Sue Ryder Foundation, caring initially for war-shattered minds and bodies in her Cavendish home but now catering for people with other disabilities in a chain of homes across the country, and abroad.

As hardline Communism began to ease, allowing contact with eastern Europe, Sue began renewing contacts with Poland, often spending days driving a lorry loaded with food from Britain to Warsaw; for this, and for other aspects of her work, she was awarded a life peerage as Lady Sue Ryder of Warsaw – and I have yet to meet a woman with more courage, drive, and perseverance than this lady who is so small you could easily not see her. Her husband became a life peer in 1991.

Sue Ryder Museum. Come to the Sue Ryder Museum beside the foundation headquarters – it's open daily 1000-1730, 80p adults; children and seniors 40p, ♿ – and see something of this remarkable woman's life, from beautiful dolls and costumes made in Poland to relics of the concentration camps, including soap made from human fat.

Sue Ryder's autobiography, *Child Of My Love,* was published by Collins Harvill in 1986.

Dukes of Devonshire. There is nothing in the village of Cavendish to tell you that this was the ancestral home of the Cavendish family, first heard of in the 15th cent and later to provide the Dukes of Devonshire. Sir John, a judge, was beheaded by the labouring classes during the Peasants' Revolt against the poll tax in 1381. His son Sir William became the first Earl of Devonshire while *his* brother George was a writer and a later Cavendish became Lord Chesham. Thomas Cavendish, the second Englishman to circumnavigate the world, belonged to the family but was born at Trimley, near Felixstowe.

Vineyard. Cavendish Manor wines are bottled at Nther Hall from 3 acres (1.2ha) of vines. Visit the cellars, vineyards, the manor house and its museum, open daily 1100-1600. ✆0787.280221.

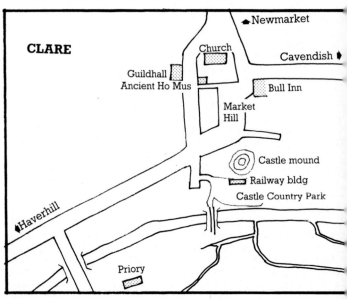

SHOPS IN CAVENDISH. Antiques, bridalwear, paintings, general store, Post Office and stationer. **Pubs:** Bull Inn, Five Bells, George, Railway Arms.

CLARE

Which mighty city gave rise to the earldoms of Hertford and Gloucester, gave its name to a county in Ireland, and produced several citizens who married into the Royal family? The answer is, of course, Clare, sometimes called the largest village in Suffolk.

Normandy. Richard the Fearless, the second Duke of Normandy, had two sons, one of whom was the father of William of Normandy, the fourth duke, who became King William I of England after 1066. Fearless Richard's other son was illegitimate, but he sired Count Gilbert de Brionne, born in 1040, and it was *his* son, Richard, *fils de* ('son of') Gilbert, who came over from Normandy to help his second-cousin William the Conqueror seize England. In return, Richard Fitzgilbert received 175 estates in the eastern counties, including the lordship of the manor of Clare. Such generosity also gave him the name of Richard de Bienfaite, 'Well-done-by.'

Clare Castle. Within a few years he began building a castle at Clare, its stone keep (the castle proper) rising from a steep earth mound piled up by his serfs. The inner and outer baileys (defensive walls) followed in the next two centuries.

Gilbert, the second Lord de Clare, founded the Benedictine Abbey of St John the Baptist in Colchester (see chapter 8) in 1095. History books record that William II, William Rufus, was killed by an arrow shot by accident or design by an unknown person in the New Forest, in August 1100, but the wall display of the de Clare family, on show in the Clare Castle Park Centre, claims that Gilbert's steward fired the arrow.

At the same time the Clare lords arrived in the Welsh Marches, soon to build the castles at Cardigan and Aberystwyth.

The second Lord de Clare died in 1115 leaving three sons, of whom Walter founded **Tintern Abbey** and Richard, the third Lord de Clare, became the first Earl of Hertford: we'll come back to him in a moment. The third son, also a Gilbert, fathered another Richard, nicknamed 'Strongbow,' who became the first Earl of Pembroke and also the man who conquered Ireland: County Clare in the west of the country bears his name to this day.

Back to Richard, Earl of Hertford. He died in 1136, the title going to his eldest son Gilbert and then to the youngest, Roger, the fifth earl.

His son Richard, the sixth earl, married Amice, great-grand-daughter of Henry I, and was one of 25 noblemen granted the privilege of being guardians of Magna Carta, signed in 1215. And why

Lavenham is a museum of medieval timber-framed houses that survived destruction.

not, for King John was Amice's brother-in-law.

Hertford and Gloucester. The seventh Earl of Hertford, yet another Gilbert de Clare, added the earldom of Gloucester and the lordship of the Marches to his titles, so that his son Richard, the *eighth* Earl of Hertford, owned vast estates in Suffolk and in his earldoms. He founded Clare Priory, to which we shall also come back.

Gilbert the Red. The *ninth* Earl of Hertford, also known as Gilbert the Red, began Caerphilly Castle in 1268, the family's strongest defence in Wales, but he is best known for attending the first proper meeting of Parliament, summoned in 1265 by Simon de Montfort. The English aristocracy was still using Norman French, as *parlement* means 'talking;' it was only the serfs and other peasants who spoke in Anglo-Saxon, which was evolving into Old English.

Gilbert the Red was the wealthiest of the de Clares, owning land in 22 English counties, in Wales, and in Ireland. In 1290, five years before his death, he married Joan of Acre, daughter of Edward I.

Joan and Gilbert had two children. Gilbert, the *tenth* earl, died at the Battle of Bannockburn in that terrible year of 1314. The crops failed, disease and famine swept the countryside – and the victorious House of Lancaster stole the estates of the defeated aristocracy, the manor of Clare going to the Mortimer family and, in the 15th cent, to the Crown.

It was the end of the de Clares as a major force in English history. But Gilbert the Red's other child, Elizabeth, having seen her husband

Hugh Despenser executed in 1326, came back to join her mother at Clare Priory. In 1338 she rescued University College in Cambridge and renamed it Clare College; her coat of arms, still on the college gate, has gilded tears to show her widow's grief. Later, however, she married Lionel, Duke of Clarence – a *Lancastrian* whose name was a corruption of 'Clare.' Their daughter married Edmund Mortimer, Earl of March, and *their* daughter Elizabeth was queen to Richard II.

Clare Priory. The priory continued until the dissolution of the monasteries and associated buildings under Henry VIII, and today's Priory House is in the restored parlour, buttery and pantry of the Eighth Earl's priory, while today's priory church was the old infirmary. And Clare Castle? Within 50 years of Gilbert's death at Bannockburn it was in ruins, and its masonry vanished centuries ago to help build the ordinary houses of Clare. Only the earth motte remains.

Railways. In the mid-19th cent the railways came to the Stour and Colne valleys. The Sudbury and Clare Railway came from Chappel and Wakes Colne, through Bures, Sudbury, Long Melford, Cavendish and Clare, to Haverhill, where it joined the Colne Valley and Halstead Railway which came from Chappel, through Earls Colne, Halstead and Castle Hedingham, to Haverhill. The S&C opened in 1860, was swallowed by the Eastern Counties Railway the next year and by the Great Eastern in 1862; the CV&H opened in 1856, was part of the ECR early in '62 and was taken over by the Great Eastern before the year was out. The London and North Eastern, the LNER, took over both lines and many others in 1921 before losing its identity to nationalisation in 1948. In the 1950s the lines were busy with freight, 80,000 sacks of grain passing through Clare station in one year.

Both branch lines closed in 1967, but while only one building remains of the S&C, the CV&H has two railway museums, as we have seen.

The one remaining building of the old S&C Railway was part of Clare Station, now the Castle Park Centre, holding a railway goods wagon and a tableau of Clare's history. The station at Clare was built within what had been the medieval inner bailey: it was the only railway station in England to be built inside a castle.

Clare Church. Richard de Clare, also known as Richard of Orbec, the first Earl of Hertford, built the Church of St Peter and St Paul on the site of a Saxon chapel, although major reconstruction around 1460 accounts for much of the present structure as well as the tower. The Flemish brass eagle-shaped lectern is one of around 40 in the country to have a slot in the beak to take coin offerings.

Maypole. At the centre of the ceiling in the south porch is the carving of a human head surrounded by leaves; this is the 'green man,' who has given his name to so many pubs in the country. He's really the tree spirit symbolising the return of summer, recalling that in pre-

Christian times the people danced around a tree; in later ages they substituted a pole and fixed the dance on the first of May.

When Cromwell's men were gaining the upper hand in the Civil Wars, his lieutenant **William Dowsing** noted in his journal on 16 January, 1643, the damage he inflicted to Clare church: "We brake down 1,000 pictures superstitious; I brake down 200; 3 of God the Father, and 3 of Christ, and the Holy Lamb, and 3 of the Holy Ghost...and the 12 Apostles were carved in wood, on the top of the Roof, which we gave order to take down."

Clare Reliquary. Edward III gave his granddaughter Philippa a necklace containing a fragment of the True Cross (see Saint Helena, chapter 8) and the rock of Calvary. It was lost in 1380, found in the ruins of the castle in 1866 and under the label of the Clare Reliquary is now on display in the church.

Ancient House. South of the church and facing its main door is a beautifully-pargeted (plastered) 15th-cent building, known as the Ancient House and now holding the town museum with exhibits from the Iron Age to the near-present. Open mid-May–end-Sep, Wed-Sat 1430-1630, Sun 1100-1230, for 60p.

Three ghosts. The Bell Hotel in the village centre grew from an ale house of 1585, which is now the reception area. It was greatly expanded to a post house in the 1750s, when the carved beams in the bar ceiling were added, taken from the priory which had recently burned down, and the 18th-cent stables were converted to bedrooms in the 1970s giving the Bell 23 rooms. But a certain highwayman doesn't like this last conversion as his ghost sometimes haunts the old stables. The ghost of an old woman visits a cottage incorporated into the hotel in the 1960s, and on rare occasions the ghost of an old man walks from the kitchen to the restaurant.

SHOPS IN CLARE. Boutiques, butcher, baker, newsagent, antiques, hairdresser, gallery, furniture, gifts, florist, fruiterer, hardware, clothes, pharmacy, bookshop, Post Office. **Pubs:** Bell Hotel, Swan Inn. **Restaurants:** Kate's tea-room, Leggeres, Peppermill.

Vineyard. Boyton Vineyard at Boyton End, Stoke-by-Clare (✆0440.61893) is open daily Apr-Oct 1030-1800. You can tour the vines, sample the wine, and have the winemaking process explained. The farmhouse gardens are also open.

8: BEYOND THE STOUR

Colchester, Harwich, Ipswich

THE LOWER STOUR is just one beautiful and historic part of East Anglia, impossible to isolate from the other regions: Breckland, the Broads, the coast, the Fens. While the area covered by this book is, for the most part, the non-tidal Stour's catchment area, I cannot ignore the major attractions beyond the next hill. So here they are.

COLCHESTER

Signs at the Colchester borough boundary warn you of what's in store, for this is Britain's oldest recorded town. Palaeolithic and Neolithic – Old and New Stone Age – relics have been found here, as well as Bronze Age tools, Celtic pottery, and early British artefacts; you can see much of it in the town's Castle Museum.

Camulodunum. The Roman governor Cunobelin, whom Shakespeare called Cymbeline, moved his administrative capital from Verulamium (St Albans) here to Camulodunum, probably because its site, on a steep hill beside the river, was easier to defend. Cunobelin minted coins here, copied from the coinage of contemporary Rome – and thousands of these have been ploughed up over the ages to lie with tons of pot shards in the museum.

The governor's death around 43AD allowed the British tribes to rebel, prompting the emperor Claudius to come over from Gaul to reimpose Roman rule. His colony at Camulodunum recalled his victory over the tribes in its name *Colonia Claudia Victricensis*, and he began building the town in a big way, adding a temple, theatre, baths and villas, none of which has left any trace above ground level. He began the **city walls,** which eventually were to reach around 1,000m east to west, 500m north to south, stretching for 1.75 miles (2.8km) and enclosing 108 acres (43ha).

Boadicea. But before the walls were finished, King Prasutagus of the Iceni died, bequeathing his territory jointly to Emperor Nero and his daughter Boadicea. The Romans seized the entire Iceni lands, forcing Boadicea to campaign for justice. Setting out from her base at what is now Exning, near Newmarket (the name is a corruption of *Iceni*), in 60, she sacked Camulodunum and other cities before being defeated by the new governor Suetonius Paulinus, and taking poison. Boadicea is sometimes called Boudicca, and you can pronounce Iceni as *eye-see-nye* or *ik-cane-ee*.

Balkerne Gate. The Romans continued building Colchester's walls, using septaria, odd-shaped lumps of calcium carbonate found naturally in London clay. Their west gate, called Balkerne Gate by the Saxons, survives as the largest Roman gate in Britain, with two roads for carriages, each 17ft (5m) wide, plus two pedestrian gates each 6ft (1.8m) wide. Large sections of the wall are also standing, some of them now incorporated in the back of the Eld Lane shopping precinct.

With the Roman province of Britannia on the point of collapse, Coel, the leader of the Britons in the area, began building his own city within the walls, calling it **Kaircoel.** By 238 Coel had added today's territories of Essex and Hertfordshire to his domains, then in 242 his wife gave birth to a daughter, Helena.

History becomes ambiguous at this point, one version claiming that Constantius Chlorus ('the Pale'), the Roman commander of Hispania (Spain), laid a three-year siege on Kaircoel-Camulodunum, beginning in 260. The siege was lifted when 18-year-old Helena agreed to marry Constantius. Their son, born in Colchester, was to become Constantine the Great.

The other version claims that the Roman Emperor Flavius Valerius Constantius laid the siege – but he would have been only 10 years old. Yet history records that it was this Constantius who married Helena and fathered Constantine the Great, and that the babe was born in what is now Bulgaria – and Constantius certainly was the Roman ruler of Britain, Gaul and Spain, and he died in York in 306.

Old King Cole. It is also fact that by 290 Coel ruled all of Britain as a Roman vassal but, as you recall a nursery rhyme about Old King Coel or Cole, I leave you to decide whether his Roman overlord was his son-in-law.

> *Old King Cole was a merry old soul,*
> *And a merry old soul was he.*
> *He called for his pipe and he called for his bowl,*
> *And he called for his fiddlers three.*

Old King Cole died in Colchester in 297, but nobody knows where he was buried.

St. Helena. The Helena who married Constantius and who was mother of Constantine the Great was – according to history – born not in Colchester but in Nicomedia, now Ismid in Turkey. It is a fact that in 326, aged 74 (which fits with her possible birth in Colchester) this Helena began a pilgrimage to the Holy Land to find the True Cross.

She allegedly stayed at Tarsus, Antioch and Lydda before finding all three of the Calvary crosses on 3 May 327. Legend attributes her identifying Jesus's cross by trying all three as a cure for a dying woman.

History takes over again in reporting her departure by sea in 327 – for where: not England? – and her stopover in Cyprus, where legend again holds sway. An angel told Helena she must build a church on the island and bless it with a fragment of the true cross. During the night a fire broke out on a mountaintop and when Helena investigated she found the cross had been transported up there and was in the fire, but undamaged.

Stavrovouni. She built the church, and the Monastery of Stavrovouni ('Mount of the Cross') that followed it still stands on that isolated Cypriot mountain top. It's the island's oldest, most remote, and strictest monastic order where women and photography are banned (see *Discover Cyprus* in this series).

Helena? She died the next year, became a saint, and now an island in mid-Atlantic bears her name. But was she the same Helena who was born in Colchester?

Colne-cester. The Saxons renamed King Coel's city 'Colne-cester, from which its present name is obvious – as well as the name of the river Colne.

Colchester's Norman castle is a museum.

A few churches were standing in the city when the Normans invaded in 1066, and the new conquerors quickly added others. In 1095 came the **Benedictine Abbey of St John the Baptist** (see Clare, chapter 7) where Catherine of Aragon stayed in 1516 on her way to Walsingham. St John's was sacked by Henry VIII, with only the gatehouse surviving, its last abbot, Thomas Beches, being hanged and mutilated in December 1539. Also around 1516 the priest Ernulph began **St Botolph Priory,** the first English home of the Austin canons. But canons and priors had a street battle in the 14th cent in which Pope Urban V had to mediate. St Botolph's was dissolved in 1536 but its ruins still stand near St Botolph's station. Botolph, by the way, began his first church in 654 in Iken, Suffolk (see *Discover The Suffolk Coast*).

The **Grey Friars** were established in town by 1279 but were ousted in 1538 with not a stone remaining. The **Crutched Friars** came in the reign of Henry III (1216-'72) but, like so many others, went in the reign of Henry VIII (1509-'47), with only the name of Crouch Street recalling their passing.

Perhaps the most unusual of Colchester's churches is **St Mary-at-the-Walls,** near Balkerne Gate, almost destroyed in the three-month Siege of Colchester in 1648, but rebuilt in 1714. Several churches are deconsecrated: St Helena's is a photographic laboratory; one is derelict, and two others are museums, detailed below.

The Castle. Colchester castle has the largest Norman keep in Europe, built on the remains of Claudius's Roman temple. The tree growing at the top of the tower in the south-west corner is believed to be a descendant of one that grew during the Civil War. The **museum** has a splendid display of historical artefacts from the area, with a leaning on Roman times. **Open** Mon-Sat 1000-1700, Sun (Apr-Oct) 1400-1700; tours of the vaults and prisons on weekends Apr-Sep, daily July and Aug; admission charged. The gardens are eyecatching, with the lower part sometimes used as the stage for the biennial **Colchester Tattoo.**

Other museums. Beside the castle stands **Hollytrees Museum,** showing mainly porcelain and fine arts, open Mon-Sat 1000-1700, free; opposite the castle is the **Natural History Museum** in a deconsecrated church, open Mon-Sat 1000-1300, 1400-1700, free; and the **Clock Museum** in Trinity St, open Apr-Oct Mon-Sat 1000-1300, 1400-1700, admission charged. **Trinity Museum,** also in a deconsecrated church in the town centre, is a craft museum, its most noteworthy wall plaque from the old days being that of General George Eliott, governor of Gibraltar during the Great Siege of 1779-'83.

The Arts. The **Mercury Theatre,** near Jumbo, stages a wide range of comedies, dramas and special events, with ticket prices ranging from £3 to £9.50; box office ✆0206.573948. The **Minories Art Gallery** is at 74 High St, near the castle; ✆0206.577067.

Boating on the tranquil Stour near Flatford.

Oyster Feast. The Romans began fishing for oysters in the Colne estuary, and Richard I gave a charter to perpetuate the rights. The modern oyster fishery has suffered pollution and competition from imports, but the molluscs are still popular whenever there is an R in the month. The Oyster Feast is held in October in the Town Hall, guests coming by invitation only.

Other Colchester attractions. The town-centre water tower, called Jumbo and now disused, has been a landmark since 1882; **Bourne Mill** was a finishing mill for bays and says (see Dedham), the cloths in which Colchester specialised with the help of Flemish weavers, many of whom lived in the much-restored **Dutch Quarter.** Come to the **Siege House** by the river and you can see the bullets that were fired into the timberwork in 1648, during the Civil War.

Out of town to the west is **Colchester Zoo** where you can pet a python, adopt a penguin and feed a seal. Open daily 0930-1730, or dusk if earlier. And to the east, on the steep Clinghoe Hill, is **Essex University,** which stages drama, music, exhibitions and other events; mailing-list information on ✆0206.873261.

TOURIST OFFICE. 2 Queen St, opposite the castle, ✆0206.712920.

Shopping. Colchester is an excellent shopping centre, competing with Chelmsford to the south-west and Ipswich to the north-east. In addition to the town centre shops there are out-of-town areas on the old bypass, Severalls Lane, and elsewhere. Parking is difficult in the centre.

Military. Colchester has one of the largest army garrisons in the country, occupying much of the southern part of town. For years, public roads crossed the camp, but the need for stricter security has resulted in several being closed.

HARWICH

Harwich is a port town on the best harbour in East Anglia with a history almost as impressive as Colchester's. In 1294 Edward I called on it to send ships to fight the Welsh, and in 1338 the French tried to burn the town at the start of the Hundred Years War. Edward III personally led 200 ships out of Harwich two years later, to victory at the Battle of Sluys.

Explorers and pilgrims. Martin Frobisher sailed from here in 1576 on his Arctic explorations, the 120-ton Harwich ship *Primrose* helped defeat the Spanish Armada, and the *Mayflower* sailed from here with a local man as master; Christopher Jones's house is at 21 King's Head St.

The first regular ferry from Harwich to the Continent sailed in 1661, but there were to be many breaks in the service; in 1672, for example, the English and Dutch fought the Battle of Sole Bay off Southwold, with the loss of the first Earl of Sandwich whose body was washed ashore at Harwich.

Samuel Pepys. The first earl was adoptive father to Samuel Pepys, the diarist, admiralty official, Master of Trinity House, and in 1673 one of two members of Parliament for Harwich when it was a 'rotten borough,' whose MPs were not elected by the people. To show how rotten things were, Pepys simultaneously won the parliamentary seat for Sandwich. You remember the third Earl of Sandwich? He was the man who put meat between two slices of bread so he needn't leave the gambling tables, thereby inventing the sandwich. He also financed Captain Cook's expedition which discovered the Hawaiian group, originally called the Sandwich Islands.

Records show that in the early 18th cent a sea passage from Harwich cost 12s 6d (62p) – but a passport cost two guineas (£2.10).

St. Nicholas's Church. The original parish church of St. Nicholas was begun in 1177 by Roger Bigod, first Earl of Norfolk, and parish rolls recall that its visitors included Francis Drake, Martin Frobisher, Horatio Nelson, James Boswell, Samuel Johnson, Daniel Defoe and, of course, Pepys. And Christopher Jones was married here twice. It was demolished in 1819 and the present church with its tall spire built, at a cost of £19,797.62p.

Harwich had two charters, from James I in 1604 and from Charles II in 1667, the second associated with the shipbuilding industry; from 1660 to 1822, 58 warships were built here, the largest being the 1,854-ton *Conqueror* in 1801.

Strange courts. James's charter established a Court of Piepowder, which could be set up at a moment's notice to try traders and peasants who would otherwise flee. The word comes from the French *pied poudré,* meaning 'dusty foot.' The Admiralty also had its own quick-decision courts (perhaps quick-justice was forfeit?) at Harwich, deciding the distribution of deodands – the word is from the French *dieu donné,* 'god given,' meaning anything which caused a person's death.

Roman cement. The coastline at Dovercourt owes its profile to the chance discovery in 1810 of an outcrop of septaria, the stone with which the Romans built Colchester's walls. As septaria can be crushed and the resulting powder mixed with water to form a cement – called Roman cement for its hardness – a cement factory opened in 1812, soon followed by another four, and over the years 200,000 tons of cliff were dug away to reach the septaria nodules. The result was the present shape of Dovercourt Bay, the southward growth of Landguard Point off Felixstowe, dredging of the harbour at a cost of £140,000, and the closure of the Old High Lighthouse.

Old High Lighthouse. The lighthouse had been built in 1818 for General Rebow who charged a penny a ton 'light dues' on all cargo entering port, but the growth of Landguard Point meant that if incoming ships lined up the high and low lights – both buildings survive – they would go aground. The 90-ft tall (27.5m) high lighthouse had a coal fire, and is one of the few such buildings with a chimney.

Redoubt. Near the old high light stands the Harwich Redoubt, a fortress 146ft (44.5m) in diameter built to defend England from Napoleon; it's among a chain of martello towers stretching from Seaford in Sussex to Aldeburgh in Suffolk.

Treadmill crane. Charles II's naval yard built a treadmill crane in 1667, a gruesome device whose lifting power came from men walking in a giant treadmill. The Romans had the first such crane in 25BC and there were many in use in medieval England, with terrible injuries possible if one man stepped out of the 16ft-diameter (4.8m) mill. The Harwich treadmill crane, working until 1927 with animal power and now resited near the old high light, is believed to be the only one in Britain and one of two in Europe, the other being in Gdansk, Poland.

Electric Palace. One of Britain's first purpose-built cinemas, the Electric Palace opened in 1911 to seat 300, closed in 1956, and was reopened in 1981 for special performances.

SHOPS IN HARWICH. Harwich and its twin town, the resort of Dovercourt, are poorly served by shops, the majority clustering around the traffic lights in the centre of Dovercourt. There are pubs aplenty. For a fuller picture of the town's story, read *The Harwich Story,* written and published by Leonard Weaver, a former mayor, in 1975.

IPSWICH

The busy town of Ipswich features in *Discover the Suffolk Coast*, but you may like to know it is the birthplace of Cardinal Wolsey who was Archbishop of York, aspirant Pope, and the power behind the throne of Henry VII; even the King of France had to bribe Wolsey with £12,000 before he could have a treaty with England. Wolsey had grand ideas about building a school and college here, but only a tiny gateway and the name of College Street survived his schemes.

Dickens came much later as a reporter on the *Ipswich Chronicle*, and the name of his famous character Pickwick is based on the old name for Ipswich – Gippeswick.

Rectory Tower (left), the Rev Edward Bull's folly at Pentlow, and Harwich's lighthouse with a built-in chimney.

9: WHEN THE SUN SETS

Where to rest your head

YOUR CHOICE OF ACCOMMODATION in the Stour valley is wide, ranging from a manor mentioned in Domesday, several haunted hotels, to bed-and-breakfast in farmhouses and private homes – or you can go self-catering.

This list is based on information gained from a variety of sources and does not claim to include everything; if *your* premises are not here please forgive me and send me details so they will be in the next edition.

The inclusion of a listing does not infer recommendation in any way, nor does its exclusion infer condemnation: information given is freely available to anybody and is correct to the best of my belief, and the absence of one of the following symbols indicates that the information, rather than the service, is lacking.

SYMBOLS:

Ø establishment's phone number
✉ number of bedrooms
▣ television lounge
✤ building is of historic or other interest
☛ tea and coffee can be made in the rooms
✕ restaurant

HOTELS

Star rating. As the tourist boards' classifications do not always correspond with other organisations' star awards, and some hotels do not publish any rating, all hotels are listed alphabetically; refer to the **postal town** for location and judge the standard by the price; tariffs, where given, are approximate base levels for a double room with breakfast.

The Angel, Market Pl, Lavenham, **Sudbury,** *Ø*0787.247388. *✉*7; 15th-cent, in town centre; £40.

The Angel Inn Hotel and Restaurant, Stoke-by-Nayland, **Colchester,** CO6 4SA *Ø*0206.263245. 16th-cent; £45.

The Bell Hotel, Clare, **Sudbury,** CO10 8NN ✆0787.277741. 🛏23; ❀ 🍷 ✗ 16th-cent.

The Bull Hotel, Long Melford, **Sudbury,** CO10 9JG ✆0787.78494; 15th-cent, with ghost.

Colchester Mill Hotel, East St, **Colchester,** CO1 2TS ✆0206.865022. 🛏58; 🆆 ❀ 🍷 ✗ overlooks quayside and river; £79.

The Crown Hotel, High St, Bildeston, **Ipswich,** IP7 7EB ✆0449.74051. 🛏15; 🆆 ✗ 15th-cent coaching inn in 2 acres; £35.

Dedham Hall, Brook St, Dedham, **Colchester,** CO7 6AD ✆0206.323027. ❀ ✗ small hotel with good restaurant; painting classes; £39.

Dedham Vale Hotel, Stratford Rd, Dedham **Colchester,** CO7 6HW. ✆0206.322273. 🛏6; ❀ ✗ in 3 acres; excellent restaurant; £87.

Edgehill Hotel, 2 High St, Hadleigh, **Ipswich,** IP7 5RJ ✆0473.822458. Family-run in period building; £33.

Gables Hotel, Angel St, Hadleigh,**Ipswich,** IP7 5EY ✆0473.827169. 15th-cent; £36.

George Hotel, 116 High St, **Colchester,** CO1 1TD ✆0206.578494. 🛏45; ❀ 🍷 ✗ 500-yr-old coaching inn; £79.

The Great House Restaurant and Hotel, Market Pl, Lavenham, **Sudbury,** CO10 9QZ ✆0787.247431. ✗ 15th-cent with courtyard and walled garden, antiques in all rooms; £68.

Hintlesham Hall, Hintlesham, **Ipswich,** IP8 3NS ✆0473.87334; 🛏33; ❀ 16th-cent mansion, £90.

Maison Talbooth, Stratford Rd, Dedham, **Colchester,** CO7 6HN ✆0206.322367. 🛏10; ❀ ✗ superb conversion of Victorian country house; £102.

Marks Tey Hotel, London Rd, Marks Tey, **Colchester,** CO6 1DV ✆0206.210001. 🛏108; 🆆 🍷 ✗; £68.

Marlborough Head Hotel, Mill Lane, Dedham, **Colchester,** CO7 6DH ✆0206.323124. 🆆 ❀ medieval wool-house; £47.

The Pier at Harwich, The Quay, **Harwich,** CO12 3HH ✆0255.241212. 🛏6; ❀ ✗ overlooks Harwich Harbour; £63.

Red Lion Hotel, High St, **Colchester,** CO1 1DJ ✆0206.577986. 🛏24; 🆆 🍷 ✗; £68.

Seckford Hall, **Woodbridge,** IP13 6NU ✆0394.335678. ❀ 16th-cent mansion; £90.

The Sun Hotel, High St, Dedham, **Colchester,** CO7 6DF ✆0206.323351. 🛏4; 🆆 🍷 16th-cent coaching in, home of my ghost Elsa; £35.

The Swan Hotel, High St, Lavenham, **Sudbury,** ✆0787.247477; 15th-cent; £95, with four-poster extra.

GUEST HOUSES, PUBS, BED and BREAKFAST

This list is compiled from tourist office information, other sources, and personal observation. It is arranged alphabetically within postal town areas which are also in abc order: Colchester, Hadleigh, Ipswich Sudbury. *The post town must be included in the address.*

116

COLCHESTER

Anderson, Mrs, 15 Roman Rd, CO1 1UR ✆0206.45154, Victorian, town centre; £28. **Bache,** Mrs, 42 Shakespeare Rd, Lexden, CO3 4HZ ✆0206.573762, no smoking; £29. **The Bauble,** Higham, CO7 6LA ✆0206.37254, country house; £35. **Bredin,** Mrs, Bovills Hall, Ardleigh, CO7 7RT ✆0206.230217, manor house listed in Domesday; £30. **Brookleigh Ho,** Alphamstone Rd, Lamarsh, Bures, CO8 5ES ✆0787.227988, modern house, £30. **Brownsmiths Fm,** Dorking Tye, Bures, CO8 5JY ✆0787.228259, working farm, £24. **Campbell,** Mrs, 4 Wavell Ave, CO2 7HP ✆0206.571736; £28. **Cedar Ho,** 16 Fiddlers La, East Bergholt, CO7 6RL ✆0206.298370, modern house; £24. **Crown & Trinity House,** 47-51 High St, Manningtree, CO11 1AF ✆0206.392620, riverside guest house in old rectory; £37. **Dundas Pl,** Colchester Rd, Ardleigh, CO7 7NP ✆0206.230625, 17th-cent; £26. **Fourbay Ho,** Cuckoo Hill, Bures, ✆0787.227082, 14th-cent. **Gladwins Fm,** Harper's Hill, Nayland, CO6 4NU ✆0206.262261, farmouse; £30. **Farthings,** Thorington St, Stoke-by-Nayland, CO6 4SP ✆0206.37338; £23. **Four Sevens Guest Ho,** 28 Inglis Rd, CO3 3HU ✆0206.46093; £28. **Hillside Ho,** Lower St, Higham, CO7 6JZ ✆0206.37264 (mobile, 0860.839633), in 16 acres; £32. **Hunt,** Mrs, 11 Newcastle Ave, Lexden, CO3 5XE ✆0206.42052; £30. **Males,** Mrs, 6 Mayberry Walk, The Willows, CO2 8PS ✆0206.43085, near town centre; £28. **Meadows,** Mrs, 102 Military Rd, CO1 2AR ✆0206.766575, Victorian; £22. **Morgan,** Mrs, 224 Maldon Rd, CO3 3BJ ✆0206.579291; £28. **Nicholson,** Mrs, 14 Roman Rd, CO1 1UR ✆0206.577905, town centre; £28. **Old Post Ho,** 10 Colchester Rd, West Bergholt, CO6 3JG ✆0206.240379; £25. **Plowright,** Mrs, 11 Harvest End, Stanway, CO3 5YX ✆0206.43202; £29. **Queen's Ho,** Church Sq, Bures, CO8 5AB ✆0787.227760, 16th-cent coaching house, £30. **Rosebank,** Lower St, Stratford St Mary, CO7 6JS ✆0206.322259, part Tudor; £28. **Rowe,** Mrs, 15 Bristol Rd, Castle Gdns, CO1 2YU ✆0206.866411, near town centre; £24. **St John's Guest Ho,** 439 Ipswich Rd, CO4 4HF ✆0206.852288, Victorian rectory; £30. **Seven Arches,** Chitts Hill, Lexden, CO3 5SX ✆0206.574896, Georgian farmhouse; £28. **Sprinks,** Mrs, Little Ho, High St, Dedham, CO7 6HJ ✆0206.322865; Georgian house, £32. **Tarquins Guest Ho,** 26 Inglis Rd, CO3 3HU ✆0206.579508; £28. **Teazles,** Stratford St Mary, CO7 6LU ✆0206.323148, period house; £25. **Thorington Hall,** Stoke-by-Nayland, CO6 4SA ✆0206.37329, 17th-cent hall, National Trust, mentioned in text; £27. **Three Horseshoes,** Church Sq, Bures, CO8 5BS ✆0787.227311, 17th-cent inn, £30. **Tuhill,** Mrs, 14 Errington Rd, Maldon Rd, CO3 3EA ✆0206.46033, Victorian; £28. **Victoria Bakery,** Heath Rd, East Bergholt, CO7 6RL ✆0206.298370, in bakery built 1897, £26. **The Vines,** 42 Military Rd, CO1 2AN ✆0206.767301; £28. **Wren Cottage,** The Street, East Bergholt, CO7 6SE ✆0206.298327 centre of village; £30. **Yeldham,** Mrs, 13 Worcester Rd, CO1 2RH ✆0206.866825, town centre; £22.

HADLEIGH

Ash St Farm, Ash St, Semer, IP7 6QZ ✆0449.741493, 15th-cent farmhouse; £28. **Benton End Farm,** Benton St, IP7 5JR ✆0473.828188, farmhouse; £22. **Howell,** Mrs, 93 Angel St, IP7 5BY ✆0473.828117, retired hoteliers; £28. **Odds & Ends,** 131 High St, IP7 5EG ✆0473.822032, 16th-cent; £30.

Prospects, Nedging Tye, IP7 7HJ ✆0449.741295, converted barn; £26.
Toppesfield Mill Ho, Tinkers La, IP7 5NG ✆0473.824097, Victorian; £22.

IPSWICH
Goodlands Fm, Raydon, IP7 5LQ ✆0473.310287, farmhouse with tennis court; £25. **Old Rectory,** Monks Eleigh, IP7 7JL ✆0449.740811, Grade II Regency in 2 acres; £40. **Red House Fm,** Kersey, IP7 6EY ✆0787.210245, farmhouse; £28. **The Shambles,** Brettenham, IP7 7QP, ✆044932.222, 4 miles N of Lavenham; £26. *Swan Inn,* High St, Monks Eleigh, IP7 7AU ✆0449.741391, 14th-cent, also ✗; £40.

SUDBURY
Birkby Cottage, 83 High St, Bildeston, ✆0449.741679; old house in village centre. **Bourne,** Mrs, Angel Corner, 17 Market Pl, Lavenham, CO10 9QZ ✆0787.247168, 15th-cent wool merchant's home; £31. **Cobwebs,** 26 Nethergate St, Clare, CO10 8NP ✆0787.277539, Grade II listed; £28. *Cock & Bell Inn,* Hall St, Long Melford, CO10 9RJ ✆0787.79807, Georgian; £40. **The Cottage,** 1 Melford Rd, CO10 ✆0787.881184, Edwardian; £22. **Crantock,** 39 Friars St, CO10 6AG ✆0787.70570, no smoking; £26. **Davis,** Mrs, 5 Priory Rd, CO10 6LB ✆0787.71088, Edwardian, no smoking; £22. **Fisher,** Mrs, 1 Westropps, Long Melford, CO10 9HW ✆0787.73660; £32. *George & Dragon,* Long Melford, CO10 9JB ✆0787.71285, country inn; £30. **Holly Cottage,** 3 Borley Rd, Rodbridge, Long Melford, CO10 9HH ✆0787.79848, 19th-cent; £25. **Ingrams Well Ho,** Ingrams Well Rd, CO10 6XJ ✆0787.73571, Victorian; £40. **Mac's Folly,** Brent Mill Dr, Brent Eleigh, CO10 9NU ✆0787.247271, period farmhouse; £32. **Meridian Cottage,** 48 High St, Lavenham, CO10 9QZ ✆0787.247923, converted barn; £30.**Mill Hill Cottage,** Glemsford, ✆0787.280721, period property. **Mill Hotel,** Walnut Tree La, CO10 0BD ✆0787.75544, converted water mill; £34. **Morley,** Mrs, 48 Water St, Lavenham, CO10 9PY ✆0787.248422, Victorian; £27. *Old Bull & Trivets,* Church St, Ballingdon, CO10 6BL ✆0787.74120, 16th-cent, former pub, now guest house and ✗; £30. **Phelan,** Mrs, 35 Gainsborough St, CO10 6EU ✆0787.881766, 15th-cent, near Gainsborough's House; £25. *Swan,* High St, Lavenham, CO10 9QA ✆0787.247477, 14th-cent; £95. **Weaver's Fm,** Bears La, Lavenham, CO10 9RX, ✆0787.247310; modern farmhouse; £30. **Westlake,** Mrs, High St Farm, Ho, Long Melford, CO10 9BD, ✆0787.75765, farmhouse; £32. **Virginia Cottage,** The Heath, Gt Waldringfield, CO10 0SA ✆0787.70878, Victorian farm cottages; £25. **Wales End Fm,** Cavendish, CO10 8DE ✆0787.280000, farmhouse; £25. *Windmill* free house, Otten Rd, Belchamp Otten, CO10 7BH ✆0787.278353, pub with ✗ and dancing; £25.

SELF-CATERING
Accommodation in these premises must be booked in advance, and the absence of a postcode means the owner is at a different address; the listing covers the entire area.

Barn Cottage, Lt Horkesley, Colchester, CO6 4DL, ✆0206.271035. **Broom Cottage,** Cherry Tree Fm, Marten's La, Polstead, Colchester, CO6 5AQ ✆0206.262387. **Corrie Cottage,** Brent Eleigh, Sudbury, ✆0787.247296.

Gladwins Farm, Harper's Hill, Nayland, Colchester, CO6 4NU, ✆0206.262261. **High St,** Lavenham; ✆0787.247777; separate owner, ✆0787.247998. **Jums Cottage,** Stoke-by-Nayland, ✆0206.262216. **Little Cottage,** Glemsford, Sudbury, ✆0787.280650. **The Old Vicarage,** Higham, Colchester, CO7 6JY, ✆0206.37248. **4 Park Gates,** Bury Rd, Lavenham, Sudbury, CO10 9RL, ✆0787.247563. **Purkis Farm Cottage,** Borley, Sudbury, ✆0787.73014. **Suffolk Country Cottages,** Higham Lodge, Higham, Colchester, CO7 6ND, ✆0206.37217. **Wissington House Cottage,** Wissington, Nayland, Colchester, CO6 4LU ✆0206.262378. **Woodstock,** Gaston St, East Bergholt, Colchester, CO7 6SD ✆0206.298724.

CAMPING

Bright House Farm, Melford Rd, Lawshall, **Bury St Edmunds,** IP29 4PX ✆0284.830385. ●Colchester Camping Caravan Park, Cymbeline Way, **Colchester,** CO3 4AG, ✆0206.45551; beside A12 bypass. ●Grange Caravan & Camping Park, East End, East Bergholt, **Colchester,** CO10 6UX ✆0206.298567–298912. ●Hideaway Camping and Caravan Site, Brent Eleigh Rd, **Lavenham,** CO10 9PE ✆0787.247.280. ●Strangers Home Camping, Bradfield, **Manningtree,** ✆0255.870304. ●Willowmere Caravan Park, Bures Rd, Lt Cornard, **Sudbury,** CO10 ONN ✆0787.75559 (Apr-Oct).

DINING

There is no shortage of places at which to eat. Fish and chips are available from Brantham to Clare, virtually all the pubs serve food, though this may range from a sandwich lunch to a four-course dinner, and there are many tea shops and middle-range restaurants.

The large towns have their selection of restaurants but if you would like a top-class meal within the villages along the Stour and its tributaries, select from Alfonso's Ristorante at Cavendish, the Angel at Lavenham, the Bull at Long Melford, the Fountain House at Dedham, the Great House at Lavenham, the Terrace Restaurant at Dedham Vale Hotel, the Swan at Lavenham, and Le Talbooth at Stratford St Mary. The exclusion of any other top-class restaurant is by error, not design.

KINGS and QUEENS of ENGLAND

from 1066 to 1901

1066–1087 **William I,** William the Conqueror, first of the Norman kings. At the end of his reign the Domesday Book is compiled, listing everything of value in the land.

1087–1100 **William II,** William Rufus.

1100–1135 **Henry I,** The Lion of Justice, younger brother of William II. Dies in Normandy.

1135–1154 **Stephen.**

1154–1189 **Henry II,** who rules most of the British Isles and half of France. Feudalism dies at the start of his reign.

1189–1199 **Richard I,** Richard the Lion-Heart or *Coeur de Lion,* goes on crusades and spends only months in England.

1199–1216 **John,** called 'Lackland' because he loses much of the French territory.

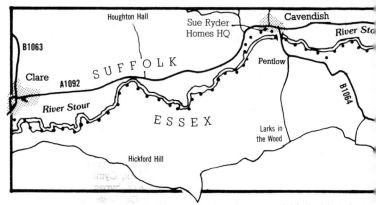

1216–1272 **Henry III,** crowned at the age of 10. In his reign Magna Carta becomes recognised as the law of the land.

1272–1307 **Edward I,** in whose reign wool becomes of major economic importance, particularly in East Anglia.

1307–1327 **Edward II,** elder son of Edward I. He is deposed in favour of his son and allegedly murdered with a red-hot poker in the anus.

1327–1377 **Edward III.** The French liaison is breaking down and in 1338 the Hundred Years War begins against France. The Black Death strikes in 1348. By 1375 England has lost all but a few towns in France.

1377–1399 **Richard II.** The first experiment with the poll tax results in the Peasants' Revolt of 1381.

1399–1413 **Henry IV,** with a weak claim to the throne, survives several battles but dies of an epileptic fit.

1413–1422 **Henry V,** who recovers some of the French provinces, dies from dysentery at Vincennes, aged 36.

1422–1461 **Henry VI** becomes king at the age of eight months. After Joan of Arc is burned at the stake the Earl of Suffolk proposes Henry marry Margaret of Anjou. In 1453 the king goes mad, shortly before the Wars of the Roses.

1461–1483 **Edward IV** succeeds from the deposed Henry while Lancaster and York continue to fight. Edward dies from pneumonia, aged 40.

1483 **Edward V** reigns from 9 April to 25 June but is victim of intrigue and dies, one of the 'princes in the Tower.'

1483–1485 **Richard III,** Edward's uncle, seizes the throne but dies at the Battle of Bosworth.

1485–1509 **Henry VII** brings in the Tudor dynasty and invades France yet again, while Columbus discovers America.

1509–1547 **Henry VIII,** the most outrageous king on the English throne, takes six wives. Because the Pope refuses to acknowledge divorce, Henry breaks from the Catholic Church and Protestantism

Concluded on page 126...

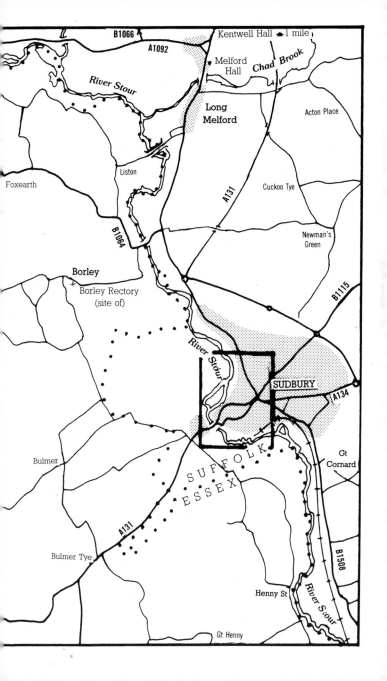

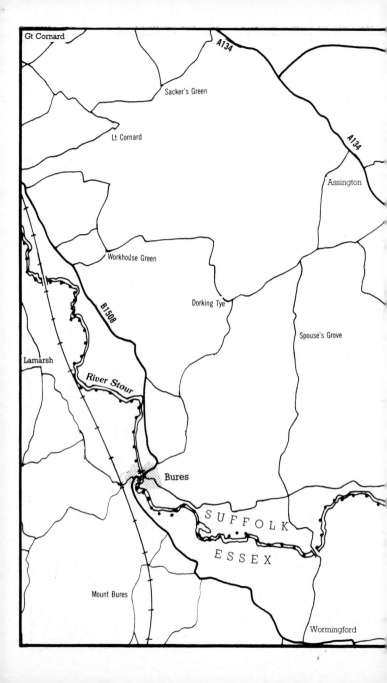

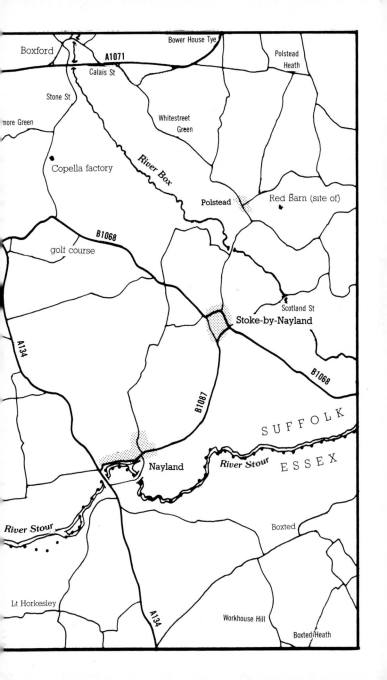

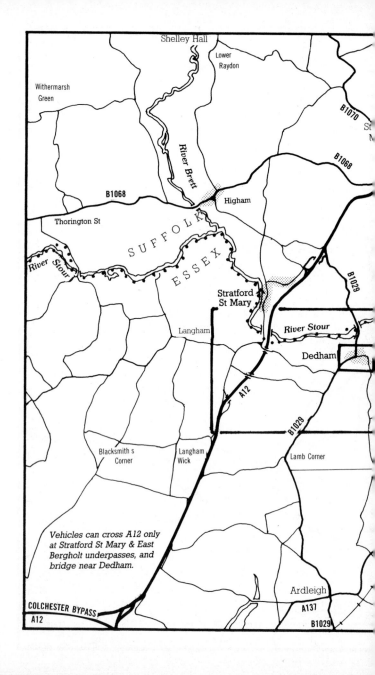

Vehicles can cross A12 only at Stratford St Mary & East Bergholt underpasses, and bridge near Dedham.

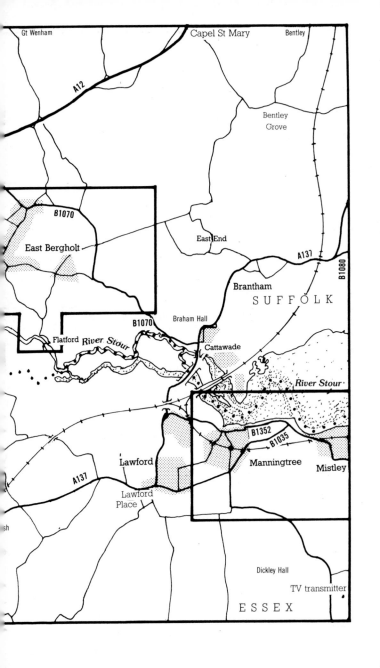

...continued from page 120.

begins. Cardinal Wolsey of Ipswich is for a while the power behind the throne. Henry dies, aged 55, from problems with his leg.

1547–1553 Edward VI, Henry's only son becomes king. The peasants revolt again in Norfolk in 1549, and Edward dies of tuberculosis, aged 15.

1553 Lady Jane Gray is proclaimed queen on 6 July but loses her support on the 19th; she loses her head the next year.

1553–1558 Mary I becomes queen while staying at Framlingham Castle, Suffolk. She marries Philip of Spain who claims the English throne – unsuccessfully. Mary dies from flu.

1558–1603 Elizabeth I, Good Queen Bess, is probably England's most charismatic queen. In her reign Drake sails around the world and later defeats the Spanish Armada.

1603–1625 James I, who is James VI of Scotland, unites the two kingdoms. Guy Fawkes tries to blow up Parliament.

1625–1649 Charles I. Charles dismisses Parliament in 1629, but it grows strong and in 1642 the Civil War starts, Parliament versus the Crown. Charles is publicly beheaded at Whitehall and the Monarchy falls.

1649–1660 The Commonwealth. Oliver Cromwell becomes Lord Protector.

1660–1685 Charles II, son of the last king, regains the throne. The Plague strikes in 1665 and the Great Fire of London destroys the city in 1666. Charles dies of apoplexy, having secretly received the last rites of the Catholic Church.

1685–1689 James II encourages Catholicism but is overthrown by a Protestant revolution.

1689–1702 William III and Mary II are offered the throne, but a Protestant succession is demanded. Mary dies from smallpox in 1694 and William rules alone.

1702–1714 Anne, daughter of James II, satisfies the legal requirement and so reigns. The 1707 Act of Union legally binds England and Scotland.

1714–1727 George I ushers in the House of Hanover. Sir Robert Walpole creates the post of Prime Minister. George has a heart attack near Osnabrück, aged 67.

1727–1760 George II. Britain expands into North America and India.

1760–1820 George III, the longest-reigning king.

1820–1830 George IV. An unpopular monarch, George dies of liver failure after too much drinking.

1830–1837 William IV dies from the same cause, aged 71.

1837–1901 Victoria, grand-daughter of George III, is the longest-reigning monarch of all, coming to the throne aged 18.

INDEX